Heaven's Hidden Frequencies

Your Guide to Discovering Prophetic Expressions of Worship

Eual A. Phillips, Jr.

Copyright Notice

Heaven's Hidden Frequencies: Your Guide to Discovering Prophetic Expressions of Worship
Copyright © 2024 by Eual Abraham Phillips, Jr.

eual.b.blessed@gmail.com

KDP ISBN:

ISBN (Paperback): 9798989212972

ISBN (Hardcover): 9798989212958

ALL RIGHTS RESERVED. This book contains material protected under International and Federal Copyright Laws and Treaties. Any unauthorized reprint or use of this material is prohibited. No part of this book may be reproduced or transmitted in any form or by any means, electronic or mechanical, including photocopying, recording, or by any information storage and retrieval system without express written permission from the author/publisher, except for the use of brief quotations in a book review.

Typefaces used in this book are Red Hat Text for text and Arvo for display.

Scripture quotations marked (NKJV) are taken from the New King James Version®. Copyright © 1982 by Thomas Nelson. Used by permission. All rights reserved.

Scripture quotations marked (NIV) are taken from the Holy Bible, New International Version®, NIV®. Copyright © 1973, 1978, 1984, 2011 by Biblica, Inc.™ Used by permission of Zondervan. All rights reserved worldwide. www.zondervan.com The "NIV" and "New International Version" are trademarks registered in the United States Patent and Trademark Office by Biblica, Inc.™

Contents

01 – What's All the Noise About?   1

02 – The Birth of Worship Arts   5

03 – Our Generational Struggle for Authentic Worship   12

04 – Counterfeit and Authentic Blueprints for Worship   14

05 – Prophetic Revelations in Worship Arts   18

06 – The Essence of Sound   22

07 – Harmonizing Your Faith with God's Timing   26

08 – Approaching Worship with Anticipation   34

09 – The Weight of Worship: Choosing the Right Songs   41

10 – Being a Sound Receiver   52

11 – Casting Crowns   61

12 – Casting Weapons   66

13 – Intelligible vs. Unintelligible Sound   73

14 – Soundscapes of Worship: Spontaneous vs. Prophetic   75

15 – Sound Amplification   80

16 – The Challenges of Navigating Spontaneous and Prophetic Sound   83

17 – The Truth Concerning Holy Spirit and Tongues   87

18 – The Sound of Motion   93

19 – The Search for Hidden Frequencies   97

20 – Worship Authority and Responsibility   104

21 – The Resonant Frequency   106

BIBLIOGRAPHY   **115**

ABOUT THE AUTHOR   **116**

ADDITIONAL BOOKS BY THE AUTHOR   **118**

01 – What's All the Noise About?

> *And when Joshua heard the noise of the people as they shouted, he said to Moses, "There is a noise of war in the camp." But he said: "It is not the noise of the shout of victory, Nor the noise of the cry of defeat, But the sound of singing I hear." (Exodus 32:17-18, NIV)*

In today's society, we are inundated with noise. We wake up to the sound of an alarm clock or a cell phone. We might be either annoyed by the sound of early morning crickets or charmed by birds chirping outside. Perhaps we wake up to sirens and garbage trucks. Maybe our neighbors played their music loudly all night. We sit down to meditate on God's word and pray, but soon the children wake up, or if you are single, a friend might text you, followed by a stream of Instagram reels. As you go about your day and finally make it to a midweek Bible study, a worship rehearsal, or a gathering at church, you eventually settle down at home. Now that you have some time to yourself, you turn on Netflix to unwind.

But have you ever stopped to ask: What did my day sound like? Every morning, we enter a battle, surrounded by the noise of war. What is this war about? It's about the prince of the power of the air bombarding you with frequencies to distract you from your true creator. When you lay down at night, have you ever wondered what the sounds or frequencies in your environment resemble? Do they convey victory or defeat?

We live in an era where discerning between sounds of victory and defeat in our expressions of worship is increasingly challenging. Sometimes, we feel that our worship accomplishes nothing. If you never experience such moments, perhaps you don't need this book, and may our Heavenly Father take you as He did with Enoch and Elijah. But for the rest of us, let's focus on the issue at hand. Worship artists, including singers, psalmists, prophetic minstrels, dancers, painters, tap dancers, mimers, and others, strive to break into heaven and bring its frequencies to earth. However, it often just sounds like noise. As we critically examine the crafted sounds and frequencies in modern worship, we question whether the lyrics are biblically accurate. But even if they are, are they culturally or contextually appropriate for the intended audience? These questions often reveal shortcomings in both spirit and truth.

Many contemporary songwriters desperately seek heavenly lyrics and frequencies at the expense of profound knowledge of God, Christ Jesus, and the Holy Spirit. They claim access to the sounds of heaven but often release noise that blurs the lines between being a believer, a Christian, and a disciple of Christ Jesus. If we're not careful, we can become captivated by how worship makes us feel rather than having an encounter with the Spirit of truth. It's no longer enough to "fact-check" or "scripture-check" lyrics. To pursue the frequencies of heaven truthfully, we must embody both Spirit and truth. We cannot call ourselves worship artists if our art lacks truth or is not spiritually founded.

Worship artists need to develop a Bible-centric and Christ-centered sense of musicality and artistry, because every artist dreams of how people will respond to their work. We create to influence hearts, minds, and movements. Artistry means nothing if it doesn't communicate or inspire those who engage with it. Just as one wouldn't hide a lit lamp under a bush, worship artists are called to shine so that people can see their work and glorify God.

Consider this: for decades, songs have gained popularity through associated dances. Social media allows movements to go viral, amplifying the impact of music. Examples include "The Twist," "Electric Slide," and "Tootsie Roll," as well as more recent trends like "Watch Me Whip/Nae Nae." These dances help embed songs in cultural memory by sparking engagement. Maybe listening to that type of music is not your testimony. Perhaps your heart was captivated as a child by the "Hokey-Pokey" or "Head, Shoulders, Knees, and Toes". Similarly, our worship reflects our response to captivated sounds and frequencies.

Heaven's Hidden Frequencies explores how we can appreciate sound as God created it and journey together as prophetic worship artists to bring heavenly frequencies to earth without compromising God's truth. This book invites you to explore worship arts from biblical, musical, scientific, and spiritual perspectives, all woven together by a chemistry teacher with experience as a church musician, intercessor, and ministry leader. I am not writing this book to impress you with knowledge but to join the Holy Spirit in waking up every worship artist seduced by false frequencies that make us appear godly but behave otherwise. This journey is meant to challenge and elevate the integrity of worshiping the Lord through artistic expression and is for those committed to serving the Lord with their artistic gifts. So, I hope you are ready for the joy and the pain associated with this journey because it's going to challenge our perceptions of worship with hard truths; but the truth will set us free!

02 – The Birth of Worship Arts

If we are going to uncover the hidden frequencies of heaven in our expressions of worship arts, we must examine the origin or the place where prophetic worship can first be observed. I'd like to propose to you that the first expression of prophetic worship in the form of musical expression took place in Exodus 15.

After being delivered from Egypt and crossing the Red Sea, Israel began to release sounds of worship in the forms of The Song of Moses and the Song of Miriam. These were not ordinary songs. Let's recall that God had been using Moses to tell Pharaoh to let Israel go so that they might worship Him, and as soon as the Egyptians were drowned, Israel automatically released their first hit single and reprise. What makes this hit single so special is that it is also prophetic, as we learn that Miriam is classified as a prophet, and it is later written that Moses is a prophet. You could even call this hit single a miracle because, for a nation that had been in bondage for over 80 years, it seems impossible for them to naturally break out into worship upon their deliverance. This song had to be supernaturally provided to them for Israel to sing unto the Lord.

The very fact that this expression of worship happened prophetically indicates one simple truth: God had gifted His children with this gift of prophetic worship prior to their deliverance. The truth is that this prophetic form of worship did not manifest until God finished His work in delivering them through the Red Sea. Prophetic worship was always intended to be a gift to humanity even before God revealed it, in the same way that God said, "Let there be light," but there was actually no physical manifestation of light until the sun, moon, and stars were given form.

Side-note: Yes, I know people want to debate this because they like to think there was a big flash of light at the beginning of creation, but the Bible does not say that the light flickered or flashed in the same way that the Spirit hovered over the waters. God said, "Let there be," and the light began its existence. If you turn off the lights in a house, it does not destroy the existence of light; the light just exists in an invisible form. Remember, the Bible is God's testimony of Himself. God is an incredible writer; why would He inspire Moses to write that the Spirit hovered but neglect to mention the flashing of light? Because God did not neglect the light; He gave it form three days later. So, back to prophetic worship. Prophetic worship always existed in the heart of God, but He was careful to write the story so that we would see an appropriate expression of it upon Israel's deliverance. God was revealing Himself to Israel through prophetic worship in the form of music.

Now that we know that Israel has a natural gift from a loving Father to break out into prophetic worship, let's fast forward a little to discuss the second birth of prophetic worship, specifically in artistic expressions other than music. In Exodus 20, Moses reveals the Ten Commandments to all of Israel before going up Mount Sinai for 40 days. Let's draw our attention to the second commandment.

If you already know the story, Israel breaks this commandment. But let's pause before making any assumptions about where this is going. Israel does not break this commandment until Exodus 32. But first, let's remind ourselves what happened in Exodus 31.

> *Then the Lord spoke to Moses, saying: "See, I have called by name Bezalel the son of Uri, the son of Hur, of the tribe of Judah. And I have filled him with the Spirit of God, in wisdom, in understanding, in knowledge, and in all manner of workmanship, to design artistic works, to work in gold, in silver, in bronze, in cutting jewels for setting, in carving wood, and to work in all manner of workmanship. And I, indeed I, have appointed with him Aholiab the son of Ahisamach, of the tribe of Dan; and I have put wisdom in the hearts of all the gifted artisans, that they may make all that I have commanded you: the tabernacle of meeting, the ark of the Testimony and the mercy seat that is on it, and all the furniture of the tabernacle—the table and its utensils, the pure gold lampstand with all its utensils, the altar of incense, the altar of burnt offering with all its utensils, and the laver and its base—the garments of ministry, the holy garments for Aaron the priest and the garments of his sons, to minister as priests, and the anointing oil and sweet incense for the holy place. According to all that I have commanded you they shall do." (Exodus 31:1-11, NKJV)*

These words were spoken about Bezalel, Oholiab, and the rest of the skilled workers before Moses came down from the mountain. The only person who heard these words was Moses. Israel had not yet known that they were being chosen to craft items with precious metals, stones, and linen. However, they knew they were not supposed to craft any images of God or a god. Therefore, we encounter another Genesis 3 moment, where humanity falls. Israel is aware of God's command not to form idols but is unaware of the plan that God has for them in the future. Israel's faith was being tested. Remember, this is the same Israel that inherently knew how to offer up prophetic worship, meaning their musicality was a gift from God. Also, remember that the gifts and callings of God are irrevocable to those who believe in Him by faith (Romans 11:28-32). Anyway, let's continue our study of this evolving story.

> *When Joshua heard the noise of the people shouting, he said to Moses, "There is the sound of war in the camp." Moses replied: "It is not the sound of victory, it is not the sound of defeat; it is the sound of singing that I hear." When Moses approached the camp and saw the calf and the dancing, his anger burned, and he threw the tablets out of his hands, breaking them to pieces at the foot of the mountain. And he took the calf the people had made and burned it in the fire; then he ground it to powder, scattered it on the water, and made the Israelites drink it. He said to Aaron, "What did these people do to you, that you led them into such great sin?" "Do not be angry, my lord," Aaron answered. "You know how prone these people are to evil. They said to me, 'Make us gods who will go before us. As for this fellow Moses who brought us up out of Egypt, we don't know what has happened to him.' So I told them, 'Whoever has any gold jewelry, take it off.' Then they gave me the gold, and I threw it into the fire, and out came this calf!" (Exodus 32:17-24, NIV)*

The worship documented in Exodus 32 is intriguing. Let me reiterate that Israel, with their gifting, automatically knew how to worship in song and dance. According to Moses's and Joshua's conversation, Israel's worship sounded like war. Today, that might be considered a compliment, but it is not, which I will explain later. However, I will commend Joshua for being a young leader with such an accurate interpretation of the sound, considering he probably had never been in a real war yet. Our seasoned leader, Moses, said that Israel's worship sounds like neither victory nor defeat. This conversation indicates that even if our sincerest worship sounds like warfare, it does not mean we are automatically victorious. This challenges the entire theology that if we fight our battles with worship, then we've already won!

There is a mentality that suggests even if we're in disobedience, worshiping hard and sincerely enough through song, dance, and art will secure our victory. Israel was trying to replicate the experience of victory in their worship. They sincerely wanted to worship God, but they were still willing to break the commandment. The sound of victory is always found in those with the greatest and most frequent expressions of Christ's obedience in their lives. Our victory is found in the obedience of one man, Jesus Christ. So His obedience must be expressed in us.

Let's shift our focus away from the music, sounds, and frequencies. We've discussed the birth of prophetic worship music, but I want to emphasize worship arts. It is easily overlooked that Israel already knew how to take metals and form them into articles of worship. Just as Israel was already gifted in prophetic expressions of worship before God called them to it, they were also blessed with the gift of craftsmanship, even though God had not yet announced this directly to them. God's call for them to be craftsmen of tabernacle furniture and their crafting of the golden calf is actually a call to worship arts. Remember, God freed them so they would learn to worship Him. Israel was so eager to answer the call to worship that they were willing to break the second commandment. This represents worship from a place of carnality and falsehood. Yet, even though Israel sinned, God did not take away their gift of crafting tabernacle items with precious stones, gems, and linen. Moses finally announces or even prophesies God's plan for Israel's gift of craftsmanship to be put into full effect in Exodus 35.

So why did God give the commandment to Israel in the first place? God gave that commandment because He knows that human beings have imaginations. He did not want humanity to create an image of Himself without His guidance. Looking at history, God created the earth and gave it to man, who fell. The only other craftsman listed in the Bible before the nation of Israel was Noah. What did humanity do next? They decided to build a tower in their name. God was amazed that humans discovered what they were capable of in unity. However, the tower was intended to make humans famous rather than God. This episode illustrates that God wanted humanity to continue revealing Himself on earth through art. Even though God did not explicitly state that He is a jealous God in the context of art until He gave the second commandment, the event at the Tower of Babel shows that God is indeed jealous when it comes to creating pieces of art intended for worship. Therefore, we must consider that building the Tower of Babel was an act of worship art because it aimed to draw people into worshiping themselves. So, while I present the idea that prophetic worship arts began with Israel, one could argue that God was reserving the appropriate time when He would interact with humanity again to create prophetic expressions of worship in the form of both music and the arts that testify of who He is in heaven.

03 – Our Generational Struggle for Authentic Worship

We have now learned that Israel is gifted by God in music, dance, prophecy, and craftsmanship. If you are not a new believer, we also know that the tabernacle furniture ultimately completed by Israel prophesied about Jesus. So now, I have to ask, what did the golden calf prophesy about Israel? Although Israel, the patriarch, struggled with God and with men and overcame, Israel, the nation, would now struggle with worship, wavering back and forth between God and idols. After all, I stated earlier that young Joshua said that Israel's worship sounded like war, and Moses reported a neutral sound in their singing.

This idea forces me to reflect on times when we, the body of Christ, may have been engaged in Spirit-filled and truthful worship that sounds like warfare, but because it was not inspired by a revelation of His victory, God was not inhabiting our praises. It's simple: God is not going to enthrone Himself on top of praises that are not inspired by an image of His victory. Yes, we know that many idolaters in Israel died when Moses returned from his ascent, but it does not alter the possible cascade of future events. It is possible that a prophetic act of worship in the form of a golden calf was released by Israel, the nation, even though Israel, the patriarch, overcame his struggles. And if Israel, the firstborn son of God, struggled with this, what makes us Christians believe that we will not struggle as well between worshiping in Spirit and in truth versus worshiping in carnality and in falsehood?

It is because the second commandment was broken that we have a generational struggle with worship. If you think we are exempt from this struggle, please go and read the entire chapter of Romans 11 because if I go any further, I will deviate from the topic of worship arts. However, this is where I hope you have not dismissed this entire paragraph. Based on the aforementioned claims, if we are not guarding our hearts in regard to worship, we will find ourselves as worship artists slipping into patterns of worshiping in carnality and falsehood, and thus, without repentance, we may prophesy ourselves into our own struggles. But again, thank God that gifts and callings are irrevocable because He remained faithful to Abraham by giving us Jesus as our Lord and Savior.

If you don't believe that the creation of the golden calf is a prophetic act that prophesies our struggle with worship, I have already provided enough present-day evidence that our generation is still struggling in its worship toward God. We have a generation of worshipers who are impatient and have not endured the Lord's discipline so that they might get a blueprint from God. Not every worship artist in our generation has been properly discipled in obtaining a blueprint. The blueprint for worshiping in Spirit and in truth is revealed to us when we obey God. When we avoid obedience to God and try to use worship arts to provoke Him into performing a sign and a wonder, we risk creating songs, choreography, and other forms of art from our own imagination of God, rather than His revelation. I pray that we would repent so that God can truly have His worship and we can truly have an accurate expression of Him.

04 – Counterfeit and Authentic Blueprints for Worship

In an age where the line between the authentic and counterfeit easily blurs, the essence of true worship stands challenged. Just as Israel crafted a golden calf out of impatience and a desire for familiarity, we too risk turning worship into a pursuit of carnal experience rather than genuine divine encounter. Worship, at its core, should reflect our profound experiences with God. Instead of seeking worship for self-gratification, we must root it in the blueprint provided by Jesus, the express image of the invisible Father. In navigating the complexities of worship today, how do we discern the genuine from the false?

Drawing from Israel's story, we understand that carnal and false worship are real concerns we must actively avoid. Israel's impatience led them to create a golden calf as they sought to reproduce a familiar sense of victory. They began to worship God not because they had experienced Him anew, but because they craved a prior triumph. This inclination towards carnal worship arises from desiring experiences rather than actual encounters with God. True worship emerges naturally after genuine experiences with God, as was exemplified when Israel crossed the Red Sea and immediately praised God for His revealed power.

This disconnect is why I am deeply concerned when modern worship teams and artists focus on songs extolling signs and wonders, asking repeatedly for God to "do something again." While I don't expect everyone to share this concern, we should be aware of the dynamics in our church services. Despite this, remember: everything works for the good of those who love the Lord. God may still perform miracles in the midst of imperfect worship to reach an earnest believer. However, we must be cautious not to misinterpret these acts as endorsements of our worship's quality, for God acts out of His goodness, not because of our worship's merit.

What then is the blueprint for worshiping in spirit and truth? It is not determined by the tempo of the song, the length of worship, spontaneous expressions, or acoustical enhancements. The true blueprint is illustrated by Jesus's life and teachings.

Consider an analogy from everyday life. When my daughter draws pictures of my wife and me, she uses a clear image of us from her memories and skills, not asking us to worship her creations. Similarly, as human parents are fully revealed to their children physically, our Father is an invisible God—a fact that complicates worship based solely on human imagination without divine guidance. Therefore, creating an image of God without His provided template tends to lead to falsehoods. Jesus, as the express image of our invisible Father, provides us with that template. His teachings remain our primary blueprint, supported by the New Testament.

The church in Corinth offers a historical lesson of its own struggle with sincere worship, akin to Israel's challenges at Mount Sinai. Paul addresses these issues in his letters, reminding us that though we live in the world, our warfare isn't waged with worldly weapons. We utilize divine powers to dismantle the strongholds of misinterpretation and misapplication in worship, ensuring every thought aligns with Christ.

We often mistakenly assume worship itself is a spiritual weapon based solely on its form or ostensible power. However, what defines a weapon as carnal or spiritual is the mindset and intent of the user. Creation, ordained by God and redeemed through Christ, remains neutral. Whether a gun or a sword, the utility for good or ill lies in the user's intent, not the object. The same truth extends to worship arts and instruments—their spirituality or carnality derives from the user's heart and perspective.

Singing, dancing, or waving flags in worship do not inherently confer holiness. Scripture reveals that we are chosen to be holy and blameless by the blood of Jesus, not by outward expressions alone. The carnal mind acts from impulse, while the spiritual mind acts from disciplined training in God's word. This disciplined approach ensures our worship is both authentic and aligned with divine truth.

Even as Paul encourages us to desire spiritual gifts, he emphasizes that our primary alignment should be with Jesus's teachings. In today's worship, there's a temptation to prioritize the manifestation of gifts over the disciplined study of Christ's teachings. Yet, authentic discipleship and freedom arise from abiding in these teachings, not merely in spiritual gifts themselves.

Ultimately, authentic worship requires us to shift from external expressions to an internal alignment with Jesus's teachings. The struggles of the Corinthian church mirror our modern challenges—issues that Paul addressed by emphasizing discipline in God's word. Worship isn't merely artistic performance; it's a spiritual engagement born of a disciplined mind. Spiritual weapons, including worship, derive their power from the practitioner's heart and mind. Our heritage as worshipers, chosen to be holy in God's sight, demands adherence to Christ's teachings above all. Thus, discernment and engagement with the word is critical, providing the true blueprint for worshiping in spirit and truth.

05 – Prophetic Revelations in Worship Arts

> *I, John, both your brother and companion in the tribulation and kingdom and patience of Jesus Christ, was on the island called Patmos for the word of God and for the testimony of Jesus Christ. I was in the Spirit on the Lord's Day, and I heard behind me a loud voice, as of a trumpet, saying, "I am the Alpha and the Omega, the First and the Last," and, "What you see, write in a book and send it to the seven churches which are in Asia: to Ephesus, to Smyrna, to Pergamos, to Thyatira, to Sardis, to Philadelphia, and to Laodicea." (Revelation 4:9-14, NKJV)*

> *Then He said to me, "Write: 'Blessed are those who are called to the marriage supper of the Lamb!'" And He said to me, "These are the true sayings of God." And I fell at His feet to worship Him. But He said to me, "See that you do not do that! I am your fellow servant, and of your brethren who have the testimony of Jesus. Worship God! For the testimony of Jesus is the spirit of prophecy." (Revelation 19:9-10, NKJV)*

To fully understand prophetic worship arts, we must recognize what Revelation 4:9 and 19:10 both tell us. When John introduces himself, he explains that he is on Patmos for two reasons: the word of God and the testimony of Jesus. He was imprisoned there because he was preaching God's word and spreading the testimony of Jesus. John was appointed to be at Patmos to receive this revelation. We have no record in the Bible of what was happening with the other apostles, but Jesus had clearly appointed John to be on Patmos to receive a revelation of Jesus that He would not grant to any other disciple to record on a scroll. John was specifically called to receive a testimony of what Jesus wanted to reveal about Himself.

When we examine Revelation 19:10, we see that the testimony of Jesus is the spirit of prophecy. Therefore, to understand prophetic worship arts, we must recognize that the spirit of prophecy must originate from what Jesus wants to reveal about Himself. Thus, if our artistic expression of worship does not allow room for Jesus to tell His own story, it becomes incredibly difficult to believe that the act is prophetic. Jesus must be in the prophecy somewhere, even if He is not explicitly mentioned.

One reason why the song released by Israel after their deliverance from Egypt can be considered prophetic worship is due to its occurrence after God revealed Himself. God had already authored the song and gave Israel the permission to release it. However, because Israel wanted to satisfy their urge to worship, they created a golden calf, which is arguably considered spontaneous praise. They did this out of a desperate desire to recreate the experience they had after crossing the Red Sea.

Yet, even though Israel sinned, God had already predestined them to use their metallurgical skills to build the tabernacle and its furniture. Today, we know that every piece of tabernacle furniture is a foreshadowing of Jesus Christ. Therefore, their metallurgy and craftsmanship could be considered prophetic acts of worship. These tabernacle articles serve as the testimony of who Jesus is and the work He would accomplish via the cross. God had a say in the writing of this testimony because He breathed His Spirit on specific individuals to carry out this work.

Even the act of writing this book, in the same way John wrote Revelation, is an act of prophetic worship manifesting through me as a teacher. Jesus has testified to me about His desire to be enthroned in our worship, and this book serves as His instruction to start the conversation within the body of Christ, a conversation that Aaron was unwilling to have with Israel when they could not wait for Moses to return with a revelation from God. Aaron missed the opportunity to recast vision to Israel and create space for God to remain first in their lives. Instead of recasting vision, he cast an image.

Therefore, if we want to have an authentic prophetic sound in our worship or pursue Heaven's hidden frequencies, we must allow Jesus to reveal Himself. We must let Him breathe His testimony on us. We must allow Jesus to cast His image in us, rather than casting our imagination onto Him. We ought to cast down imaginations, not project them on Christ. The problem with our worship today is that we want God to breathe on us for reasons that have nothing to do with how He wants to reveal Himself. Even when we sing songs filled with scripture, it sometimes feels as though we are prescribing to God what we want Him to be, instead of allowing Him to prescribe the word that will transform us into the image of His Son.

In conclusion, we must remember that Heaven is constantly responding to the fully revealed Jesus. Thus, to produce the frequencies of Heaven on earth, we must respond to a revelation of Jesus, rather than simply to how we inaccurately imagine Him to be. It is our response to what Christ wants to communicate about Himself to the church that makes our worship arts prophetic. This is what it means for the spirit of prophecy to intersect with worship arts.

By embracing this understanding, worship artists—whether singers, dancers, musicians, mimers, poets, or painters—can truly align their creative expressions with Heaven's purpose. This alignment allows the profound echoes of Heaven, the prophetic expressions of faith, to resonate on Earth. Our task is not just to create, but to listen, to receive, and ultimately to reflect the divine revelation that Jesus imparts to each of us.

06 – The Essence of Sound

In order to comprehend the hidden frequencies of heaven, we are going to begin this journey from the beginning of creation. We will examine how God embedded frequency in creation. Then we will work our way back toward Christ who is seated in heaven. First, when the spirit of God hovered over the waters, hovering automatically indicates vibrational frequencies. When God created the light, separated the light from the darkness, and described the conclusion of the first day, God had set an appointed time for light to appear according to a schedule. The use of the word day implies frequency or that time would begin to repeat itself in a cycle.

Imagine a quiet room where you can almost hear the silence. Then, suddenly, a gentle hum starts to fill the space, growing louder and richer. This hum, this sound, is more than just noise; it is "the mechanical radiant energy that is transmitted by longitudinal pressure waves in a material medium (such as air) and is the objective cause of hearing," as Merriam-Webster puts it. Essentially, sound is pressure exerted on any state of matter—solid, liquid, gas, or even plasma. For some, this might be a revelation, a concept that wasn't part of their schooling, but indeed, sound impacts everything it touches.

Think back to your science classes, where we learned about the states of matter. Solids, for example, aren't as immovable as we might think. On a molecular level, solids vibrate in place, holding tightly to each other, much like a well-rehearsed dance troupe. They're compressible, moldable, and strongly attracted to one another, akin to magnets. Liquids, on the other hand, flow and rotate around each other, separating more easily because their mutual attraction is less intense. Gases, the wildest dancers of all, prefer their independence, colliding with each other at breakneck speeds in an elastic motion. Each state of matter—solid, liquid, gas—is made up of atoms, and sound, this radiant energy, applies pressure on these atoms. Sound can travel through any medium, making it a versatile and omnipresent force. We must understand that when God spoke in Genesis 1, He was applying mechanical and radiant pressure on the earth to launch the earth toward an equilibrium that is aligned with heaven. For our discussions throughout this book, we'll mainly focus on the gaseous state when we talk about atmospheres.

To deepen our understanding of how sound exerts pressure on atmospheres, let's turn to a familiar biblical analogy—the potter and the clay.

> "Then the word of the Lord came to me. He said, 'Can I not do with you, Israel, as this potter does?' declares the Lord. 'Like clay in the hand of the potter, so are you in my hand, Israel. If at any time I announce that a nation or kingdom is to be uprooted, torn down and destroyed, and if that nation I warned repents of its evil, then I will relent and not inflict on it the disaster I had planned. And if at another time I announce that a nation or kingdom is to be built up and planted, and if it does evil in my sight and does not obey me, then I will reconsider the good I had intended to do for it.

> *'Now therefore say to the people of Judah and those living in Jerusalem, "This is what the Lord says: Look! I am preparing a disaster for you and devising a plan against you. So turn from your evil ways, each one of you, and reform your ways and your actions." But they will reply, "It's no use. We will continue with our own plans; we will all follow the stubbornness of our evil hearts."'" (Jeremiah 18:5-12, NIV)*

Imagine the potter at work, skillfully sculpting a piece of clay, shaping and molding it with precise, deliberate movements. Similarly, dancers and musicians sculpt the atmosphere with their art. The potter's material is clay—solid, tangible. For the dancer and musician, their material is the air, the atmosphere around them, which is a gas. They operate with a different state of matter but share the same intention and skill in their craft.

Now, let's delve into the concept of breath. According to Merriam-Webster, breath is "air filled with a fragrance or odor." This definition reminds us that the air around us is not as ordinary as we might think. We often take breathing for granted, yet the air we breathe carries fragrances that can transform our experience. Just as a potter's hands shape the clay, our worship can captivate the air, turning it into something divine. All of creation, as commanded in Psalms 148 and 150, is called to worship the Lord. As a dancer or worship artist, your movements infuse the air with a fragrance that becomes breath, praising the Lord. This connection explains why "everything that has breath" praises the Lord—everything in creation has the capacity to worship. We are designed to be captivated by God, and our movements in worship, whether dance or any other form, are vital in this divine interaction.

Think about your daily life. Whether you're a musician, dancer, psalmist, or even a bread baker, your work influences the atmosphere. A baker's movements fill the air with the fragrant scent of freshly baked bread and pastries. Every action that involves movement releases a fragrance into the atmosphere, drawing creation's attention and captivating it. Our work, our worship, exerts pressure on the atmospheres around us, creating a space where the divine and the mundane meet. And yet, God chose to hide frequencies in each piece of creation that uniquely points back to him.

07 – Harmonizing Your Faith with God's Timing

There is a time for everything and a season for every activity under the heavens:

a time to be born and a time to die,
a time to plant and a time to uproot,
a time to kill and a time to heal,
a time to tear down and a time to build,
a time to weep and a time to laugh,
a time to mourn and a time to dance,
a time to scatter stones and a time to gather them,
a time to embrace and a time to refrain from embracing,
a time to search and a time to give up,
a time to keep and a time to throw away,
a time to tear and a time to mend,
a time to be silent and a time to speak,
a time to love and a time to hate,
a time for war and a time for peace.

What do workers gain from their toil? I have seen the burden God has laid on the human race. He has made everything beautiful in its time. He has also set eternity in the human heart; yet[a] no one can fathom what God has done from beginning to end. I know that there is nothing better for people than to be happy and to do good while they live. That each of them may eat and drink, and find satisfaction in all their toil—this is the gift of God. I know that everything God does will endure forever; nothing can be added to it and nothing taken from it. God does it so that people will fear him. (Ecclesiastes 3:1-14, NIV)

In the dance of life, timing is everything. This timeless wisdom from Ecclesiastes reminds us that every moment has its purpose. When we worship, whether through dance, music, or song, we are engaging in an act that reflects this profound truth. As worship artists, we are given a song, a rhythm, and a sequence of notes, and it is up to us to decide how to move within that allotted time. Every beat, every pause, and every movement carries meaning. What will we accomplish within the timing of the music? What burden will God lay upon us as we express our worship? What beauty will we create with the time we have in the song? What aspects of eternity does God want us to portray in our worship?

Developing sensitivity to the timings of music is essential because there is a timing to everything. To maximize the time and space that God has provided for us to worship in, we must educate ourselves, become skilled, and be well-versed in musicality. Let's take a moment to humble ourselves and refamiliarize ourselves with some fundamental musicality terms to enhance our understanding and sensitivity to music and worship.

An Overview of Basic Musicality Terms

A beat is defined as "a division or unit of musical time in a measure" (Kuhn, 1999, 99). The most common number of beats in a measure of music is four. For worship artists, whether singers, dancers, musicians, or others, the beat serves as the primary reference from which they decide how to perform—

either aligning with the beat or intentionally moving against it, depending on the creative expression required (Grant, 2017).

The meter is defined as "the pattern in which a steady succession of rhythmic pulses is organized… one complete pattern or its equivalent in length is termed a measure or bar" (Randel, 1986, 489). At a composer's discretion, music can have multiple beats per measure. The most common meter is "4/4 time," which means there are four beats per measure, with the quarter note as the dominant beat. When performing in the style of a waltz, it typically adheres to a "3/4" meter, with three beats per measure. Other less common meters, such as "5/4" and "7/8," contribute unique characteristics to a song, influencing artistic performances.

Tempo, defined as "the specific speed at which music is performed" (Latham, 2002), is measured in beats per minute (bpm). For worship artists, mastering varying tempos enhances listening skills and control over their expressive abilities, allowing them to adapt and perfect the quality of their movements or musical expressions (Grant, 2017).

Accent in music refers to "the first beat of each measure is the strong beat and thus carries a metrical accent" (Randel, 1986, 3). It serves to keep performers alert. For musicians, if they lose their place while sight-reading, they should look for the rhythm's accent or first beat to regain their position.

Duration, defined as "the time that a sound or silence lasts" (Randel, 1986, 247), is important for worship artists who often learn choreography or musical pieces in segments. With musicality, it's beneficial to match movements with the duration of musical phrases. This integration results in a flow that appears seamless and continuous to the observer (Grant, 2017).

Articulation describes "the way notes are joined to one another when forming a musical line, e.g., staccato, legato, tenuto, glissando, slur, phrase mark, accents, sforzandos, rinforzandos, etc." (Dolmetsch Online Music Dictionary, 2015a). Proper articulation embeds expressiveness into music, enriching its composition (Grant, 2017).

Rhythmic variation, defined as "the disposition of strong (or accented) and weak (or unaccented) beats in a piece of music" (Dolmetsch Online Music Dictionary, 2015c), includes syncopation, where accents are placed on sub-beats and off-beats. This variation allows multiple choreographed rhythms to coexist within a musical phrase, adding complexity as it requires changes in the duration of movements on accented and unaccented beats.

Finally, a canon is a musical form where "a (second, third, fourth, etc.) line starting later than the one before it matches it note for note, overlapping the parts" (Dolmetsch Online Music Dictionary, 2015b). Similar to a round like "Row, Row, Row Your Boat," a canon enriches the listening and visual experience by prompting artists to develop aural, proprioceptive, and spatial awareness through overlapping phrases (Grant, 2017).

Be Sober and Sensitive

> "Be very careful, then, how you live—not as unwise but as wise, making the most of every opportunity, because the days are evil. Therefore, do not be foolish, but understand what the Lord's will is. Do not get drunk on wine, which leads to debauchery. Instead, be filled with the Spirit, speaking to one another with psalms, hymns, and songs from the Spirit. Sing and make music from your heart to the Lord, always giving thanks to God the Father for everything, in the name of our Lord Jesus Christ." (Ephesians 5:15-20, NIV)

Having gone through these musicality terms, I challenge you to no longer be unwise but to be rich in wisdom concerning every movement you make in your dance, every note you play, and every song you sing. Do not allow your worship to be a sloppy byproduct of insensitivity to the musical timings God has created for you to participate in. Be filled with the Spirit, and stay sensitive to the psalms, hymns, and songs from the Spirit. When God signals a song to be sung from heaven, it is because He desires to bring people into a higher life of sobriety. He is trying to captivate people with a song. Therefore, I encourage you to take up the responsibility of being a visual and auditory expression of the music that He provides from the high life of heaven. Discern the times within the music and worship!

In embracing this call, remind yourself that faith embodies complete confidence in the workings of God's power, securing the anticipated outcomes He has destined. As worship artists, our artistry is bound to this divine timing, where each note, movement, and expression is guided by a sacred tempo gifted from the foundations of the earth. By aligning our expressions with this divine rhythm, we elevate our worship, ensuring it becomes a powerful conduit for God's message and presence.

The Divine Equation: Time and Power

In physics, power is the force applied over time to move an object. In spiritual terms, power is the manifestation of God's will moving through us across the stages of life He has orchestrated. How often do we cry out to God, "How long?" Only to forget that time itself is a profound gift. Genesis tells us that God created the sun and the moon to mark sacred times (Genesis 1:14-19, NIV). God, in His infinite wisdom, gifted time to humanity—believers and non-believers alike—to set the tempo for our devotion and service.

Faith, Power, and Worship

As worship artists, understanding that faith requires confidence in God's unseen power underscores our creative expressions. When we perform, our faith and artistry are tested across time. How effectively we harness our work in song, dance, word, and art depends on our respect for the divine equation of time and power. This respect is crucial in enhancing performance and impacting our audience, fostering a sacred atmosphere through which God's power can be revealed.

Respecting Time in Worship

To begin accessing heaven's hidden frequencies, we must learn to respect time again. Time is a gift from God and was established when God spoke, "Let there be light." Both light and sound are measured in time, marking the divine schedule God had in mind. In worship settings, consider these concerns:

- To respect time, we must not rehearse by accident or neglect the looming presence of our worship services where God desires to make His presence known.
- A lack of respect for rehearsal time risks missed divine moments and the opportunity for spiritual awakening and emergence from darkness.
- Disrespecting time leads us to miss opportunities to reinforce, reinvigorate, reignite, and restore the saints with spiritual songs, hymns, and melodies. Overlooking notes, rhythms, tones, and phrases can hinder the spiritual atmosphere we seek to create.
- Power in physics derives from time, just as God gave time to enable power to flow. Squandering this gift delays the manifestation of power from heaven into earthly realms.

To truly resonate with heaven's hidden frequencies, worship artists must embrace and cherish the sacredness of time. Our creative acts are not bound by earthly constraints but are opportunities for divine encounters. In this understanding, respecting time becomes a form of worship itself, aligning our creative expressions with God's eternal schedule.

When we combine what we understand about time with the fact that breath is air with a fragrance, as defined by Merriam-Webster, we can come to a profound understanding. The wisest thing we can do with our time is to use or release the Breath, which is His Spirit, that He has given us—not only to worship Him in song and dance, but as we live and move and have our being in Christ throughout the entire day. Imagine your every action of worship being a 24-hour musical score that applies pressure on the atmosphere around you and is a fragrance unto the Lord. One of the reasons why God gifted humanity time was to see what melody man would synthesize using His Breath. In every note, movement, and expression, let us use the time He has given us to create a symphony that honors Him.

08 – Approaching Worship with Anticipation

One day I was invited to a recording session, but not as a musician. I was invited as an intercessor. It was a little awkward at first because I'm not used to being a bystander at a recording studio. However, I had to trust that the Lord had me on assignment. As I was praying, I was prompted to write down the prayers as led, beginning with Romans 8:19-22 (NKJV) as the inspiration.

> *For the earnest expectation of the creation eagerly waits for the revealing of the sons of God. For the creation was subjected to futility, not willingly, but because of Him who subjected it in hope; because the creation itself also will be delivered from the bondage of corruption into the glorious liberty of the children of God. For we know that the whole creation groans and labors with birth pangs together until now.*

In this heartfelt prayer, I invite the presence of God into the recording studio, imploring Him to sanctify every piece of equipment and each artist involved. The prayer envisions the recording process as a sacred act, where cameras, microphones, and even the very frequencies of sound are aligned with divine purpose. I ask for the unity of artists, engineers, and technicians under the guidance of the Holy Spirit, ensuring that every note and beat carry the transformative message of the gospel. The prayer resonates with the hope that these sacred sounds will pierce darkness, touch hearts, and echo the glory of God's kingdom, ultimately declaring salvation and the new covenant through Christ.

As you read this prayer, I urge you to see it not as a teaching or a new philosophy but as a revelatory prayer. Throughout this book, I will confront and challenge many philosophies and teachings about worship that are either inaccurate or incomplete. This prayer is meant to free your spirit from broken philosophies, allowing you to reimagine what God aims to accomplish through your prophetic expressions of worship. We've all been guilty of imitating philosophies without understanding them, inhibiting God's vision for what He desires to do. Therefore, read this prayer not as an absolute truth, but as a fresh discovery of God's desires for worship arts, rather than an imposition of my will on music recording session.

This deeply spiritual approach positions every aspect of the recording process as an offering of worship, urging participants to fully embrace their roles with divine reverence and anticipation, free from preconceived notions that may hinder the true purpose of worship.

1: Father, I thank You and praise You for giving this recording studio and its equipment an anticipation for the glory that Your sons and daughters are going to deposit through song.
2: Thank You for allowing the recording equipment to become divine co-participants in heralding the message of the gospel in the recording session.
3: May every camera capture the image of the Son in our recording artists.

4: May every camera and electronic device serve their purpose in capturing the visible image of our invisible Father and our Savior who sits on the throne.

5: Unify the voice of every singer and the limbs of every musician, dance artist, and visual artist.

6: May every piece of equipment humble itself under the glory of the King.

7: May not one part of the recording and electrical body exalt itself over any other parts.

8: May every equipment be appropriately engineered, balanced, and calibrated for its appropriate consumption of shared power.

9: May every voice and instrument be calibrated to the winds and frequencies of the Holy Spirit.

10: We prophesy to the four winds to breathe life over all of the dry bones and dry sound equipment in this worship space.

11: Let all of the sound equipment spring to life and awaken to the message and the wind of the Holy Spirit.

12: May the Spirit hold together every cable and line just as every joint and ligament are joined together.

13: May every frequency in the forms of hertz, cycles, and spins be calibrated with the rejoicing, leaping, and spinning of worshippers and creatures found in heaven.

14: May every chip, soundboard, and processor be baptized in the knowledge of Christ so that each piece of equipment may successfully comprehend and convert the message of the gospel found in the worship music.

15: May the sound engineer receive the peace necessary to produce holy and pleasing results from the music recording.

16: May the sound engineer's mind be freed from the enslavement of any other projects and ideas that would interfere with the mixing and recording processes.

17: May there be a clear execution of the software and hardware.
18: May even the engineer be fully captivated and instructed by the Holy Spirit and the sounds of heaven echoing through the chambers and booths of the recording studio.
19: As each chord progression advances, may heaven manifest itself and make further progress into the earth.
20: Just as the mighty rushing wind of the Holy Spirit found the upper room in the book of Acts, I pray that Your Spirit would rush into the recording chambers with a sound that will refresh the hearts of the recording artists, engineers, and technicians.
21: May the gospel message in the music be clearly heard with language that ignites the hearts of the artists and potential listeners.
22: May Your breath move through Your artists and cause them to synchronously navigate through the recording session.
23: May Your inexpressible joy be upon the faces of our recording artists as they communicate notes and transitions to one another.
24: May every string and drumbeat carry the strength to sustain the message communicated through the musicians.
25: We thank You for every metallurgical and chemical process that was used to create all of the equipment to capture a glimpse of the incomparably great power that You have for those who will come to believe in this gospel message.
26: May the bass instruments begin to release the thunder of God's throne and activate every order and judgment that will condemn the frequencies of hell.
27: As the pianists and string players strike their chords, may arrows of light begin to pierce the darkness and puncture

the depths of every human heart who hears the chord progressions of heaven.

28: We declare that there is no more delay concerning the frequencies required of this recording session and that there would be no signal jams between the recording studio and heaven.

29: Strengthen the frequencies of this music recording for future generations.

30: Sustain the frequencies as You sustain the sun's rays.

31: We pray that You will cause the song recorded in this studio session to be evidence of the new wine that is being poured out for those who will show up to feast with our Lord and Savior, Jesus Christ.

32: May this recording be evidence of new wine imbued with an ancient and enhanced flavor that overtakes listeners with peace, joy, and righteousness in the Holy Spirit.

33: We thank You for every son and daughter who will accept the invitation to the banquet and taste of this new wine of the kingdom being poured out through this recording.

34: As the song is being electromagnetically recorded, captured, stored, and rendered, may Your power go to work to develop the intense and deep flavor of the wine within this recording.

35: We thank You for every future that You are redeeming through this song by the power of Jesus's shed blood.

36: Thank You for every life You are preserving with this song according to Your infinite wisdom.

37: We declare that salvation belongs to the Lord and may the message of Your salvation in this song begin to saturate the sounds of this recording session.

38: Father, we ask that You would be the invisible string that ties together every chord progression in this recording session.

39: May the chord progressions tug on the hearts of listeners and lead them into greater commitments to sanctification.
40: May the mind of every recording artist be freed from enslavement and free to vocalize and instrumentalize the work and the message that they have been called to herald.
41: We declare that all of the instrumentation is answering its call to fulfill its purpose that has been established by You through Your holy children.
42: We thank You for every listener who has been called and predestined to hear the good work produced in this gospel recording.
43: We thank You for every piece of equipment that is responding to Your demand that Your sons and daughters have placed on them to capture the gospel message in this recording session.
44: And it is in the name of Jesus that we pray; amen.

Remember, when God left the earth under man's care, the expectation was that all of creation would no longer answer to God, but rather to the sons of God. This includes the sound equipment. Secondly, the next time you read through the book of Revelation, read it as all of heaven worshipfully responding to the fully revealed Jesus Christ. Additionally, when God created the heavens and the earth, those two realms responded to Him in worship.

Therefore, I hope that as a worship artist, this prayer has redefined your perspective of your position or role in your worship arts team. Even if you are a dancer, do you not expect the floor to respond to your feet so that you do not slip and fall because your eyes are more steadfastly fixed on Jesus than

Peter's were when he was invited to walk on water? Even if you are a prophetic painter, do you not expect the canvas and the colors to respond to the Christ within you? When you begin to meditate on the idea that all of creation is waiting to respond to Christ in us, will you continue to take your position as a worship artist in vain? In all, I hope that you will approach every future worship set with greater anticipation than any of your former worship sets.

09 – The Weight of Worship: Choosing the Right Songs

In the realm of worship arts, the selections we make as artists—be it songs, movements, or expressions—hold the power to transform spiritual and physical atmospheres. This chapter explores the profound impact of song selection on worship environments, guiding artists such as singers, musicians, dancers, painters, and poets in aligning their creative choices with divine intent. By examining the types of pressure exerted on atmospheres, the challenges in choosing the right song, and the importance of mature spiritual discernment, we aim to equip worship artists with the insight needed to craft experiences that honor God and inspire the congregation. As we delve into these themes, consider how the melodies and words you choose can serve as vessels of truth, shaping the hearts and spirits of both performers and observers alike.

Defining Song Selection

In worship arts, song selection can be defined as the intentional choice that influences both the physical and spiritual atmosphere. It was previously mentioned that the potter uses a pottery wheel in the same way a worship artist uses a song. We have this solid state that can be molded, reshaped, or reformed on a spinning wheel. Placing the clay on the spinning wheel gives the potter greater control over its formation. Similarly, the song applies pressure to the atmosphere, causing air molecules to align with the frequencies emitted by your sound system. Thus, these tools prepare the environment for receptivity to your expressions.

When the potter places the clay on the wheel and spins it, manipulating the clay becomes easier; the clay becomes more responsive to the potter's touch. This is akin to what happens with songs. You begin to shift the atmosphere in such a way that the air becomes more responsive to your expressions, as it seeks to carry the fragrance of worship. Air becomes breath when it carries fragrance. In worship, the air becomes a conduit for the fragrance released by your worshipful movements, thus becoming breath. Therefore, song choice is crucial when aiming to be a vessel that transforms the atmosphere.

Types of Pressure in the Bible

There are two types of pressure that can be exerted in atmospheres and on other objects. The first is the weight of sin.

> *"Therefore we also, since we are surrounded by so great a cloud of witnesses, let us lay aside every weight, and the sin which so easily ensnares us, and let us run with endurance the race that is set before us." (Hebrews 12:1, NKJV)*

Notice that sin is a weight that can be set aside. Sin has the ability to hinder our movements. It prevents individuals from developing the endurance necessary to appropriately apply their faith toward God.

Within the same scripture, the writer gives us a good reason why we need to cast off the weights of sin. Previously, I mentioned that the atmosphere will respond to your movements and carry the breath of worship generated from your movements. The writer mentions the cloud of witnesses. We should want to cast off the weight of sin because of the cloud. We have to develop a consciousness of the fact that we have an audience in heaven that is watching and cheering us on in our race. We need cloud consciousness if we want to worship God without the weight of sin.

The second pressure is the weight of God's glory.

> *"For our light affliction, which is but for a moment, is working for us a far more exceeding and eternal weight of glory, while we do not look at the things which are seen, but at the things which are not seen. For the things which are seen are temporary, but the things which are not seen are eternal." (2 Corinthians 4:17-18, NKJV)*

Even God's glory has a weight to it, and it can actually activate or suspend our movements, depending on what God wants to do with His glory. We need momentary light afflictions in our lives in order to prepare us for the movements that God wants us to perform in our worship. This weight of glory is not meant to oppress and hold us back but rather trains and disciplines us to have supernatural endurance, which is what the weight of sin tries to prevent us from attaining.

Keeping these two types of weight in mind, here are two questions for you:

- What type of sound captivates you? (Instrumental music is no exception!)
- What type of pressure do you want to exert on the atmosphere as you worship?

The Challenges of Song Selection

I highly advise that you question where songs come from. If they are not coming from the right place, then people will be captivated by the wrong spirit. Let's review a song that can be used as an example of the importance of song selection because people can have varying opinions and arguments about the interpretation of this song's lyrics.

> *"Before I spoke a word, You were singing over me.*
> *You have been so, so good to me.*
> *Before I took a breath, You breathed Your life in me.*
> *You have been so, so kind to me.*
> *Oh, the overwhelming, never-ending, reckless love*
> *of God!"* (Asbury, Reckless Love, 2018)

Did you notice anything that could be wrong with the song? The potential problem with the song is the use of the word "reckless" to describe God's love. Do not miss the intent behind what is being said. This is not an attempt to slander Cory Asbury, the writer, or question his walk with God. I am 100% positive that Cory Asbury meant well when he used the word "reckless" to describe God's love. My intent in all of this is not to condemn you if you differ in opinion but rather that you would become more thoughtful about who God is.

If we educate ourselves, we will realize that reckless means "marked by lack of caution; irresponsible" (Merriam-Webster). This is not an accurate description of God's character. Let's refer to the scriptures to get a more accurate glimpse of God's love.

> *"For He chose us in Him before the creation of the world to be holy and blameless in His sight. In love, He predestined us for adoption to sonship through Jesus Christ, in accordance with His pleasure and will..." (Ephesians 1:4-5, NIV, 2011)*

According to Ephesians, God's love is not reckless. He planned for us all to be here with all of His wisdom. This is the type of love where someone makes plans to spend the rest of their life with another, similar to a marriage covenant. Reckless love lacks a clear plan for the future and direction for those involved in this pseudo-covenant. This type of love resembles the love we may have tried to imitate before knowing God. Even though God loves the world, He does not love the world with the world's definition of love. Reckless love implies irresponsibility and a lack of caution for the other individual involved. Reckless love permits someone to freely leave a relationship when the person selfishly does not get what they expect from the relationship or if there is a strong offense between the two.

God's love is a profound truth that ought not to be distorted. If any word could be used to replace reckless, the next best fit would probably be radical, but I am sure radical just does not fit the meter of the song as well as reckless does. Anyway, this is why we must be careful of the songs that are chosen for worship, even if the person is a reputable Christian. We must check them ourselves. When we worship, we must ensure that all the music we use aligns with the heart of God, the word of God, and the knowledge of God.

Taking Songs into Captivity

In order to check our songs, we must first take songs into captivity. Music not only can be used as a weapon to destroy strongholds, but it can lay down foundations for new ones. Not every stronghold is bad. If we are the temple of the Holy Spirit, then we ourselves are being built as a stronghold. We must study our songs. We must be yoked to the song. The song must have us in captivity, and we must have the song in captivity. This is a symbiotic relationship, similar to how God wants us to be in supernatural unity (John 17:20-24).

> *"For the weapons of our warfare are not carnal but mighty in God for pulling down strongholds, casting down arguments and every high thing that exalts itself against the knowledge of God, bringing every thought into captivity to the obedience of Christ..." (2 Corinthians 10:4-5, NKJV)*

We are supposed to take every thought and imagination and present it to Christ, including songs. If you practice this, it will make you a more sensitive worshipper. By simply practicing the discipline of taking a song to Him and allowing Him to decide whether the song selection is worthy enough to represent Him, you will be more readily used by God in shifting the atmosphere and bringing the atmosphere into obedience. In other words, before we can bring an atmosphere into obedience, we must present to Him the tools, the songs, the equipment, the choreography, and ourselves for obedience to Christ. Attempting to shift atmospheres without obedience and submission to Christ has several consequences for the ego that will not be explored at this moment.

Maintaining the Standards of Song Selection

In 2019, I attended a worship conference and asked one of the session leaders their opinion on music or songs that have erroneous language, such as "Reckless Love." I asked that question because I was taught that songs can disciple generations of people, which is true; we are still being discipled by David's psalms to this day and are composing countless arrangements using scriptures across the entire Bible. As a teacher, I wanted to ask the hard question about "Reckless Love" because I was truly convicted.

This worship leader replied by saying that English is a primary example of a language that is always changing the meaning of words. He even said that 20 years from now, Merriam-Webster could add a definition of reckless that includes being an exuberant lover of God. Often in other languages, the meaning of words does not change when translated.

One of the things I do not like to do with people is debate with them over their beliefs. I prefer to hear their beliefs, go to God, and then allow God to reveal the truth to me. This is what Paul writes in 2 Corinthians 10:4-5. Jesus also recommends this in John 7:16-18. So to avoid debate, I accepted what I believed to be his opinion at the time, thanked him for his response, and sat down.

After spending time with God, I developed a defense against such an argument presented by the worship leader. If we can change the meaning of any word, then that means the words of men are fallible. The word of God is infallible and does not change. This implies that the words of men are subject to lies, deceit, and corruption, whereas God's word is incorruptible truth. God's identity cannot be wrapped up in lies or misconceptions because our concept of Him often affects our faith in Him. If we can simply change the meaning of things instead of exploring the deep truths and their existing definitions, then this can ultimately lead to licentiousness. This mentality can even encourage believers to misinterpret scriptures because they might have changed the meaning of the word of God to make it relevant to their personal context or imagination, rather than interpreting God's word based on the context it was originally in and then comparing it to other instances in the Bible. We have often associated licentiousness with sexual immorality and other obvious sins, but we neglect the idea that licentiousness can occur with the application and misuse of God's word being wrapped up in our own vain imaginations.

Let's examine an additional argument that was brought up at the worship conference I attended. If you consider a new convert, they might say that God's love is reckless because God risked everything to save them. The argument continued on the premise that reckless could be used as slang, similar to how people use "wicked cool," "mad stupid," or "stupid cool." No matter what generation you are born into, slang vocabulary is often commonly used by teenagers and young adults. If the individual matures beyond the young adult stage, they will not find themselves using slang anymore to describe life. They will describe life accurately and for what it truly is. Even for someone who is educated like me, I would hope that the word reckless, as slang, would simply phase out of my vocabulary. As a more mature person, I now begin to associate reckless behavior with the past, such as making poor and selfish decisions in life, like having too much wine to drink. Reckless is also typically associated with negative behavior. Yes, there are negative consequences that the Father outlines throughout the Bible, but the Father does not exhibit negative behaviors. Otherwise, He would lose His right to be called Father.

After having a conversation with the Father, here is what He said to me from the perspective of being a teacher:

> "So Christ Himself gave the apostles, the prophets, the evangelists, the pastors, and teachers, to equip His people for works of service so that the body of Christ may be built up until we all reach unity in the faith and in the knowledge of the Son of God and become mature, attaining to the whole measure of the fullness of Christ. Then we will no longer be infants, tossed back and forth by the waves, and

> *blown here and there by every wind of teaching and by the cunning and craftiness of people in their deceitful scheming. Instead, speaking the truth in love, we will grow to become in every respect the mature body of Him who is the head, that is, Christ. From Him, the whole body, joined and held together by every supporting ligament, grows and builds itself up in love, as each part does its work." (Ephesians 4:11-16, NIV)*

Since every believer has to start somewhere in their faith, it is acceptable for someone who is new and immature to have a perspective of God's love as being reckless. God is incredibly merciful and patient with us regarding how we have perceived Him in error in our relationship with Him. However, every believer is called to a mature and correct perspective of God at some point in time. The long-term goal of maturity cannot be lowered or negated, but at the same time, it's okay to lower the barrier to entry based on the believer's state of mind.

One of the reasons why the body of Christ has not reached maturity is because we hold on to antiquated and immature mindsets of who God is. There is a tendency for members of the body to think of God the same way they did when they first got saved; they may have been saved for ten or twenty years and have not made significant advancements in knowledge of our Lord and Savior, Jesus. Our revelation and love for Jesus should be getting deeper, longer, wider, and higher than it has ever been in the past. Our perception of God becomes simplified and complex at the same time, but ultimately, it becomes fully developed.

As a teacher, my greatest desire is for my students to reach full maturity. If a believer's best descriptor of God's love is still rooted in the word "reckless" after being saved for 10-20 years, then they have not progressed toward the whole measure of the fullness of Christ. For someone like myself, who is a seasoned believer, using the word reckless is a regression of my revelatory knowledge of God. It is the equivalent of how the Jewish people studied the law of Moses, the Ten Commandments for centuries, but when Jesus said, "Love your neighbor," the people responded by saying, "Who is my neighbor?" Their revelation of God had become completely stagnant because they never realized that the law of Moses was pointing to God's love. Their antiquated mindsets prevented them from receiving Jesus. Likewise, we should not allow antiquated thoughts to become strongholds that prevent us from receiving the fullness of God.

Therefore, song selection is important. The song you choose could be communicating something that you do not want to communicate. The song could be setting up an atmosphere that caters to immature believers but does not advance the knowledge of Jesus in such a way that produces maturity within the body of Christ. Who is your audience? Who will witness your ministry to God? This is what you must think about because your ministry will apply pressure not just on the atmosphere but also on people's spirits and souls.

10 – Being a Sound Receiver

In the symphony of worship, every artist—from singers and musicians to dancers and poets—plays a vital role in orchestrating a divine resonance that reverberates through the spiritual and physical realms. This chapter explores the profound impact of sound and vision in worship, uncovering the ways in which they influence both the atmosphere and the hearts of believers. By examining key biblical encounters, we delve into the powerful interplay between holy fear and divine expression, drawing insights for today's worship artists. As we journey through the stories of Goliath's intimidating roar and the awe-inspiring voice of Jesus, we will discover how the sounds of our worship can either paralyze with fear or empower with faith. Embark on this exploration to refine your craft, resonate with the sound of heaven, and transform the world through your divinely inspired artistry.

We are all like tuning forks; we resonate and respond to sounds and pressures that are exerted on us. When a baby cries, it exerts pressure on the parents to meet its needs. Surveys say a baby's cry is one of the most provoking sounds in the world. Although it can be incredibly annoying, the child has an innate power to release a sound that captivates the parents and prompts them into action. Scratching a chalkboard produces a sound that sends a chill down the spine of anyone nearby. If you've ever been in a technologically deprived classroom, you know this sound. It provokes a physiological response from our bodies. All these different sounds affect particle movement down to the atomic level.

The Sound of Unholy Fear

> *A champion named Goliath, from Gath, came out from the Philistine camp. His height was six cubits and a span. He wore a bronze helmet and a coat of scale armor weighing five thousand shekels; on his legs were bronze greaves, and a bronze javelin hung on his back. His spear shaft was like a weaver's rod, and its iron point weighed six hundred shekels. His shield bearer went ahead of him.*
>
> *Goliath stood and shouted to the ranks of Israel, "Why do you come out and line up for battle? Am I not a Philistine, and are you not servants of Saul? Choose a man and have him come down to me. If he is able to fight and kill me, we will become your subjects; but if I overcome him and kill him, you will become our subjects and serve us." Then the Philistine said, "This day I defy the armies of Israel! Give me a man and let us fight each other." On hearing the Philistine's words, Saul and all the Israelites were dismayed and terrified. (1 Samuel 17:4-11, NIV)*

Let's examine the pressure Goliath exerted on Israel through sound. He spread fear and paralysis over the warriors of Israel. In the spirit, Goliath's words become a repetitious and poisonous song in our hearts. We become filled with condemnation and fear. This example shows that sound has both physical and spiritual impacts on our movements. Therefore, it is important to heed what you hear and how you hear it because it can affect your ability to move with the Holy Spirit in your worship art form.

When we examine the events, Israel first saw Goliath. Then Goliath spoke a message that Israel heard. It wasn't the sight of Goliath that produced fear; it was hearing Goliath's message. In the flesh, vision influences your perception of sound. As worship artists, we know there is a warfare component to our worship. We cannot be captivated by the sound of fear because it will paralyze our true and proper worship to God.

The Sound of Holy Fear

> *On the Lord's Day, I was in the Spirit, and I heard behind me a loud voice like a trumpet, which said: "Write on a scroll what you see and send it to the seven churches: to Ephesus, Smyrna, Pergamum, Thyatira, Sardis, Philadelphia, and Laodicea."*
>
> *I turned around to see the voice that was speaking to me. When I turned, I saw seven golden lampstands, and among the lampstands was someone like a son of man, dressed in a robe reaching down to His feet and with a golden sash around His chest. The hair on His head was white like wool, as white as snow, and His eyes were like blazing fire. His feet were like bronze glowing in a furnace, and His voice was like the sound of rushing waters. In His right hand, He held seven stars, and coming out of His mouth was a sharp, double-edged sword. His face was like the sun shining in all its brilliance.*
>
> *When I saw Him, I fell at His feet as though dead. Then He placed His right hand on me and said: "Do not be afraid. I am the First and the Last. I am the*

> *Living One; I was dead, and now look, I am alive forever and ever, and I hold the keys of death and Hades.*
>
> *"Write, therefore, what you have seen, what is now and what will take place later. The mystery of the seven stars that you saw in my right hand and of the seven golden lampstands is this: The seven stars are the angels of the seven churches, and the seven lampstands are the seven churches. (Revelation 1:10-17, NIV)*

When we examine the events between Jesus and John, we find a contrast. First, Jesus speaks, and then John hears. John turns to see the voice and breaks out into holy fear. Unlike the scene with Israel and Goliath, the Lord uses sound to direct our gaze. The critical thing to pay attention to is the source of the sound. In this case, it was the Lord Jesus in His heavenly glory. Therefore, a sound from heaven exerts pressure that induces holy fear. When we are captivated by the fear of the Lord, this fear prepares us to be messengers of the mysteries of God, as evidenced by Jesus instructing John to write the book of Revelation.

The Power of Resonating in Holy Fear

While certain forms of worship, such as dance, produce inaudible sounds to the human ear, vision remains crucial. With Israel and Goliath, sound reinforced the vision. In the encounter between Jesus and John, the vision affirmed what was heard. Though the outcomes differ, both events highlight a vital truth:

when vision and sound align, they evoke a powerful response from witnesses.

Returning to the encounter with Goliath, let's examine what happens when someone who resonates with the holy fear of the Lord steps onto the battlefield.

> *When Eliab, David's oldest brother, heard him speaking with the men, he burned with anger and asked, "Why have you come down here? And with whom did you leave those few sheep in the wilderness? I know how conceited you are and how wicked your heart is; you came down only to watch the battle."*
>
> *"What have I done now?" said David. "Can't I speak?" He then turned to someone else and brought up the same matter, and the men answered him as before. What David said was overheard and reported to Saul, and Saul sent for him. (1 Samuel 17:28-31, NIV)*

Notice what happens when David steps onto the scene. It is evident that the people on the battlefield were consumed by fear and did not want David to speak. Additionally, the voice of fear tried to send David back to where he came from as if David was an irresponsible worker who would risk his responsibilities for glory. However, even though they tried to silence David's sound, a word still got out to Saul about David's rebuke against the Philistines. Let's examine the words of the man who spent time with God in the wilderness.

> But David said to Saul, "Your servant has been keeping his father's sheep. When a lion or a bear came and carried off a sheep from the flock, I went after it, struck it and rescued the sheep from its mouth. When it turned on me, I seized it by its hair, struck it and killed it. Your servant has killed both the lion and the bear; this uncircumcised Philistine will be like one of them because he has defied the armies of the living God. The Lord who rescued me from the paw of the lion and the paw of the bear will rescue me from the hand of this Philistine." (1 Samuel 17:34-37, NIV)

Notice the language that David uses in describing the history of victories against animals in the field. David begins sharing his testimony in the first and third person, using words such as "I" and "your servant." Even after David said that he himself was the one who killed both the lion and the bear, he closes his testimony by saying that the Lord rescued him. This is how a man of God, who has spent time worshipping and growing in the holy fear of the Lord, speaks. He speaks as if he is one with the Father, similarly to how Jesus often speaks in the gospels.

> Then Saul dressed David in his own tunic. He put a coat of armor on him and a bronze helmet on his head. David fastened on his sword over the tunic and tried walking around because he was not used to them. "I cannot go in these," he said to Saul, "because I am not used to them." So he took them off. Then he took his staff in his hand, chose five smooth stones from the stream, put them in the pouch of his shepherd's bag and, with his sling in his hand, approached the Philistine. (1 Samuel 17:38-40, NIV)

Saul's attempt to dress David in his armor is quite significant. If David had secured a victory in Saul's armor, people probably would have thought that it was Saul who killed Goliath, not David. These pieces of armor physically weighed David down. However, on the spiritual side, the armor applied more pressure on him to suppress the sound that was in him. Even from a physics perspective, when a soldier wears a helmet over his head, usually the helmet covers a significant amount of the face, which changes the sound of the person's voice. This helmet literally could have changed the sound of David's message even if he had made it to the battlefield. Anyway, both Saul and the armor had been sitting under the sound of unholy fear. For David to wear the armor, he would be clothing himself in unholy fear. This armor would have hindered the execution of God's judgment against the Philistines. Thankfully, the holy fear of God did not allow David to wear this unholy armor.

Now pay attention to what David did next. Armed with a staff and a sling, David went to a stream and chose five smooth stones, placing them in his shepherd's bag. I would argue that these five smooth stones had been sitting under the sound of rushing waters, which could be associated with the sound of the Lord's voice in heaven (Ezekiel 43:2; Revelation 14:2). If this comparison of the stream to the Lord's voice is valid, then those stones were already captivated by Jesus and submitted to Him. This action is significant because David brought tools that had already been consecrated or submitted to God. He approached the battlefield with tools that resonated with the same sound he developed in the fields with the animals. Now let's proceed to analyze David's message before his victory over Goliath.

> *David said to the Philistine, "You come against me with sword and spear and javelin, but I come against you in the name of the Lord Almighty, the God of the armies of Israel, whom you have defied. This day the Lord will deliver you into my hands, and I'll strike you down and cut off your head. This very day I will give the carcasses of the Philistine army to the birds and the wild animals, and the whole world will know that there is a God in Israel. All those gathered here will know that it is not by sword or spear that the Lord saves; for the battle is the Lord's, and He will give all of you into our hands." (1 Samuel 17:45-47, NIV)*

David endured several events aimed at contaminating the sound he had developed so that the atmosphere would not submit to God. David declared that Goliath came with weapons, but he came to the battlefield in the name of the Lord Almighty and with an anointed message. David's sound not only set Israel free but also set all of creation free. David was not just speaking to Goliath; he was speaking to every created thing. He even informed the animals, likely terrorized by the Philistines, that they too would receive a reward by feeding on the carcasses of the Philistines. David released a sound that recaptured the attention of creation and turned it against the Philistines. Creation had been held captive by the Philistines for so long that it was groaning for the manifestation of a son of God (Romans 8:21-22). On that day, that son was David.

After learning of David's experience with Goliath from a different perspective, I hope you are beginning to understand and value the concept of the sound of your worship. Worship doesn't always involve music, but all worship generates a sound that captivates creation. Creation will recognize this sound and try to join in worship with you. David may have been singing in the fields as he shepherded animals, but his shepherding itself can be considered worship as well. When you do anything with gratitude unto the Lord, it is worship that carries the sound of heaven—the sound of the Chief Shepherd, who is Jesus, accompanied him onto the battlefield against the Philistines.

Overall, everything about you needs to be captivated by God and be a revelation of the Lord Jesus. Therefore, I leave you with this final statement: the degree to which you are captivated by God will also be the degree to which the atmospheres will be captivated and shifted by you.

11 – Casting Crowns

Before the throne, there was a sea of glass, like crystal. And in the midst of the throne, and around the throne, were four living creatures full of eyes in front and in back. The first living creature was like a lion, the second living creature like a calf, the third living creature had a face like a man, and the fourth living creature was like a flying eagle. The four living creatures, each having six wings, were full of eyes around and within. And they do not rest day or night, saying:

"Holy, holy, holy, Lord God Almighty, Who was and is and is to come!"

Whenever the living creatures give glory and honor and thanks to Him who sits on the throne, who lives forever and ever, the twenty-four elders fall down before Him who sits on the throne and worship Him who lives forever and ever, and cast their crowns before the throne, saying:

"You are worthy, O Lord, To receive glory and honor and power; For You created all things, And by Your will they exist and were created." (Revelation 4:9-10, NKJV)

This chapter contains the primary revelation that inspired the title of this book. If you are reading this, perhaps you are already familiar with several songs that contain lyrics that paint a picture of the events that occur around the throne in Revelation 4. You've heard the song about the four creatures. You might have even sung a few songs that contain Revelation 4:8 in their lyrics. I often hear people preach about participating in worship alongside the 24 elders casting their crowns before the throne. But now, I need you to close your eyes and ask you to replay this scene in your holy and sanctified imagination. Now open your ears. What else do you hear when you read the passage? Did you ever think to pay attention to what a sea of glass, like crystal, might sound like? In Revelation 15, the sea of glass has fire mingled with it. Have you considered the frequencies of sound emitted from a sea of glass mingled with fire? Did you notice what the wind may sound like as it rustles through the wings of the four living creatures? But have you ever considered the sound of a cast crown?

Now come back to earth and imagine sneaking into the kitchen at night to get yourself a midnight snack. You open the cabinet and begin to carefully pull out a plate. However, you make a severe miscalculation in the strength required to free your chosen plate from captivity in the cabinet, and the plate falls to the floor and begins to rattle and spin as your heart literally skips a beat because you're hoping that the noise does not wake up anyone else in the house. Or perhaps you are watching one of your favorite medieval fight scenes only to find that the sword of your favorite character clashes to the ground, signaling his unexpected defeat. Whether or not you have developed a frame of reference for the sound of metal clanging on the floor, I still highly suggest that you go on social media, such as YouTube, and search for a video demonstration of Euler's Disc. Seriously, put this book down and go watch a video. Now begin to imagine all the music and singing that takes place out of synchrony with the sounds of casting crowns into the sea of glass mingled with fire. The frequencies released by the crowns as they are cast into the sea of glass are among the hidden frequencies of heaven that we may ignore because the sound of metal clashing to the ground does not sound heroic or glamorous to our flesh. Perhaps we need to embrace the possibility that frequencies meant to irritate our flesh may actually be a highly valuable and fragrant sound to God, our Father, and our Lord and Savior Jesus Christ!

So what does this hidden frequency of heaven found in the cast crown mean? To extract this meaning, we must examine both the cast crown itself and the people responsible for casting the crowns: the elders. The casted crown is a symbol of either a completely surrendered life or a life that perpetually casts down every authority and anxiety that tries to rule over it. David was adept at casting his cares and anxieties on the Lord, which probably played a role in him being a great psalmist. Check out this scripture:

> *Search me, O God, and know my heart; Try me, and know my anxieties; And see if there is any wicked way in me, And lead me in the way everlasting. (Psalm 139:23-24, NKJV)*

Oftentimes, we are unskilled in how we cast our anxieties onto the Lord.

To get the second meaning behind the hidden frequency of heaven found in the cast crown, we must look at who is casting the crowns: the elders. The title of elder in the Bible refers to someone who has overcome temptation. This is where David failed. David was willing to have a man killed to cover up his love affair with Bathsheba. Even when his children were out of control under his kingship, David did not do anything to curb the temptations that lured his children into sin. Do you now understand why the sound of the cast crown is irritating to our flesh and pleasing to our Father, who is Spirit? Anytime we need to overcome temptation, it's going to influence our flesh. It not only affected David's flesh, but it also affected his own children. David did not fully surrender his life to the point of resisting temptation and helping his children learn to resist their temptations.

One of the things that have been grieving my spirit is who leads me in worship. At first, I thought I was being incredibly judgmental. I try to be very careful about how I speak of leaders because I often tell people, you don't know what it takes to wear that crown or to bear the burden of leading people as a pastor, or a worship leader, which is true in many circumstances. However, I had to face a certain fact in this new generation of worshippers. A large number of our most popular worship songs are empty of power because they are either being sung or written by people who have not overcome temptation. Many of these worship artists say that they are overcoming their enemies with worship, but when they step off the stage, they are still battling temptations with depression and anxiety. How can this be? Someone must be lying. Again, if we consider David, being a great worship artist, it did not help him win his battles against temptation. So how can worship leaders claim that their worship is their weapon against the enemy while still being afflicted with so much anxiety? The answer can be found in the Greek word for "cast," which is "ballo," the word that is used for ballistics, such as archery, catapults, cannon fire, and gunfire. To cast an object means to throw or let go of something without caring where it falls. It includes turning our cares over to the point that we don't even care about the uncertainty of the results. It also means to pour out, like rivers of water.

We are casting our cares and anxieties in ways that are ineffective for our spirits. Instead of casting our cares and anxieties to our heavenly Father, we are casting our cares and anxieties into our weapons that we claim to use for worship and into our crowns to affirm our position in the structure of our local churches.

12 – Casting Weapons

For though we live in the world, we do not wage war as the world does. The weapons we fight with are not the weapons of the world. On the contrary, they have divine power to demolish strongholds. We demolish arguments and every pretension that sets itself up against the knowledge of God, and we take captive every thought to make it obedient to Christ. And we will be ready to punish every act of disobedience, once your obedience is complete. (2 Cor. 10:3-6, NIV)

We have stepped into a doctrinal error that worship is a spiritual weapon. We think that what makes a weapon spiritual or carnal is the design or the manifestation of the weapon. That is not true. All of creation is subject to man, as ordained by God in Genesis 1, and upon the redemption of creation through Christ Jesus. For example, a gun is a weapon that can be used for good or for evil. A sword is a weapon that can be used for good or for evil. The weapons are neutral. So what makes a weapon carnal or spiritual is the mindset and motivation of the man who uses the weapon. Thus, if we transfer this truth into the worship arts, what makes the weapon carnal or spiritual is whatever sound the user has been captivated by. The instrument or weapon of choice takes on the nature and purpose of its user.

This means that singing a worship song can be done with a carnal mind or a spiritual mind. This means that dancing and waving a flag can be done with a carnal or a spiritual mind. Yes, I said it. Just because you sing a song, dance a dance, or wave a banner has no power to make you holy. The scriptures say that we were chosen to be holy and blameless before the foundations of the world to be holy in God's sight. We became holy by the shedding of Jesus's blood. We do not become holy just because we utilize our worship artistry.

The carnal mind causes an individual to act and perform from the place of undisciplined instinct. The spiritual mind empowers an individual to act and perform from a place of disciplined training. But what must we be disciplined and trained in? It must be the Word of God. If you are undisciplined in the Word of God, then the lack of discipline will be observed in your sound. Everyone may not be able to detect it, but someone else who is more skilled and disciplined in both the Word and in the execution of the gift will sense it.

Let me give you an example of a disciple who went from being undisciplined to becoming an elder and even defined what it means to be an elder: Peter. Remember in the garden of Gethsemane when Jesus took Peter, James, and John off to pray, but the disciples kept falling asleep? Look at Jesus's response:

> *"Then He came to the disciples and found them sleeping, and said to Peter, 'What! Could you not watch with Me one hour? Watch and pray, lest you enter into temptation. The spirit indeed is willing, but the flesh is weak.'" (Matthew 26:40-41, NKJV)*

Peter, even though a disciple, was still undisciplined in his discipleship with Christ to pray against temptation. As a result of not being prepared in the place of prayer, he gives into the temptation of the arrest by cutting off a man's ear (John 18:10). Peter acted on instinct and not by the Holy Spirit. He still had very little faith in what Jesus had testified about himself even though Jesus told his disciples what was going to take place. He was captivated by Jesus, but not yet captivated by Jesus's teachings. Peter was always anxious about Jesus dying from the moment he tried to rebuke Jesus for saying such things. Even just before Jesus went to the cross, Peter still had not cast his anxiety about Jesus's death onto the Father. Instead, he cast his anxiety into his sword and cut Malchus's ear off. The name, Malchus, means kingdom. Therefore, this is what we do with our carnal worship when we say worship is our weapon, but we have yet to fully cast our cares and anxieties on the Lord: we end up cutting off the ears of those in the kingdom who need to hear heaven's hidden frequencies. Fellow worship artists, we owe it to ourselves and to God's elect to ensure that we are not contaminated with our anxieties because the very gifts that God has given us to liberate people will actually keep them in darkness. But, thankfully, Jesus was still there to restore healing to the kingdom. Please don't get discouraged. Jesus can heal. But I still don't want to be the one chopping off people's ears in the spirit.

Yet, after the horrific incident in the garden, Peter still became an elder.

> *"The elders who are among you I exhort, I who am a fellow elder and a witness of the sufferings of Christ, and also a partaker of the glory that will be revealed: Shepherd the flock of God which is among you, serving as overseers, not by compulsion but willingly, not for dishonest gain but eagerly; nor as being lords over those entrusted to you, but being examples to the flock; and when the Chief Shepherd appears, you*

will receive the crown of glory that does not fade away." (1 Peter 5:1-4, NKJV)

Based on this scripture, we now come back to the crown. This indicates that Peter had finally learned how to cast his cares and anxieties on the Father. He understood the authority and influence that he possessed in Christ and was committed to stewarding that authority correctly. Peter learned how to become a worshipper who not only knew that he would receive a crown, but who would not be ashamed to remove it like the elders described in Revelation 4. Peter had finally learned a lifestyle of worship that was completely surrendered to God.

I want to make an analogy to fiction to help us deeply understand why God requires us to carry the sound of a cast crown. In the "Lord of the Rings" series, an evil being creates the rings of power that would allow him to enslave every humanoid species and rule Middle-earth by their capitalizing on different manifestations of addiction to power, such as healing, money, strength, wisdom, and so forth. However, the real test of temptation in the series is not about resisting putting the ring on. The harder temptation was always to take the ring off. Like the ring, the crown is a symbol of what a person depends on to exercise their authority and dominion in their realm of influence.

So as a worship artist, if you can cast your crown, then that means you are more committed to surrendering your power and authority in exchange for the kingdom of God to come through you! King Saul had a kingdom stripped from him because of his disobedience, even though he could musically prophesy anytime he was around prophetic musicians. Saul was addicted to his influence as a king and did not want to imagine the kingdom coming through anyone else even though he was disobedient. This is where we fail as worship artists. Sometimes, we don't want to imagine that the kingdom will come or manifest without us. Thus, we become addicted to becoming the lead soloist in music, song, dance, and mime while we are losing battle after battle with temptation. We need to learn to cast our crowns before God on a regular basis in prayer because the sound of surrender that emanates from a cast one of heaven's hidden frequencies pertaining to worship arts.

So what happens when we refuse to cast off our crowns? In "The Lord of the Rings," the one ring must be destroyed in the fires of Mount Doom, symbolizing the need to rid oneself of the addiction to power and control. If we are unwilling to surrender our crowns—our symbols of power and authority—to God out of fear of losing them, we risk being enslaved by them just as the one ring enslaves its wearer. Your surrendered crown serves as proof that you cannot be tempted and that your faith has been tested and purified, which makes you an elder in the spirit.

Now let's tie this to scripture:

> "You have heard that it was said to those of old, 'You shall not commit adultery.' But I say to you that whoever looks at a woman to lust for her has already committed adultery with her in his heart. If your right eye causes you to sin, pluck it out and cast it from you; for it is more profitable for you that one of your members perish, than for your whole body to be cast

> *into hell. And if your right hand causes you to sin, cut it off and cast it from you; for it is more profitable for you that one of your members perish, than for your whole body to be cast into hell."* (Matthew 5:27-30, NKJV)

While this scripture refers to sexual adultery, it is possible to commit adultery or to lust after our positions as worship artists. In lusting after these positions, powers, titles, thrones, and crowns, we can feel important, thinking that we are ruling and reigning with Christ, but in reality, we are being ruled by the crown in the same way the people of Middle-earth were ruled by the rings instead of patiently waiting for the crown that the Father wishes to bestow upon us! We may not be losing against the temptation of sexual immorality, but we might lose to temptation when a brother or sister in Christ disrespects our leadership titles or the manifestation of our gifts. We might be defeated by the temptation of slandering or gossiping about someone when we think we've been treated unfairly. Christ is looking for a group of true worshippers who are not just going to sing the perfect harmonies and frequencies of heaven but those who carry the frequencies of heaven in their hearts that empower them to overcome every type of temptation just as He has.

Therefore, if we do not learn how to cast these crowns before the Father in heaven, we will certainly risk experiencing our own destruction and demise when someone, or even God, forcefully humiliates us and removes our crown, causing us to lose our entire life. Surrendering our crowns so that we can avoid the temptation is essential to accessing the hidden frequencies of heaven in our worship arts. Therefore, resist every earthly award with confidence in your heavenly crown. If you resist the frequencies of temptation, you will carry and resonate with the frequencies of the holy priesthood and nation!

13 – Intelligible vs. Unintelligible Sound

> *Now, brothers and sisters, if I come to you and speak in tongues, what good will I be to you, unless I bring you some revelation or knowledge or prophecy or word of instruction? (1 Corinthians 14:6, NIV)*

Let us begin to dive into the concept of intelligible sound. Like speaking in tongues, anything that produces a sound must carry some type of meaning or message; otherwise, the utterance is completely useless to humanity. The sound ought to come packaged with revelation, knowledge, prophecy, or a word of instruction.

> *Again, if the trumpet does not sound a clear call, who will get ready for battle? So it is with you. Unless you speak intelligible words with your tongue, how will anyone know what you are saying? You will just be speaking into the air. (1 Corinthians 14:8-9, NIV)*

What Paul was ultimately saying is that the intelligibility of sound affects movement execution. If the trumpet sound is not clear, then the execution is hindered. There is confusion, and people cannot go to battle or into war properly. Imagine if the sound of a fire alarm was replaced with the sound of a chirping bird. No one would think to exit the building to escape the fire until they either smelled smoke or the fire reached the room where the people are. By then, you could almost say that it is too late to safely escape in a calm and orderly fashion. Whenever there is a sound that is not properly assigned or clearly communicated, there is room for confusion. It hinders our physical movements just as Goliath's sound paralyzed Israel.

On the other hand, when Jesus speaks, He is really trying to stir up a movement in you. Therefore, we can define intelligible sound as the mechanical radiant energy that applies pressure on an atmosphere and motivates its listeners into decisively organized action.

When I was in the marching band in high school and college, the most important thing to do first is to learn the music before going out to the football field to lay out drill and choreography. By intimately knowing the music first, I became more confident in carrying out my instructions on the football field. Combining the music with my movements helped me discern where I needed to be positioned on the football field. Pretty soon, the number and size of the steps I needed to take would be embedded into the music that I learned.

To this day, I can still visualize where I was on the football field when I recall the music that was played. Likewise, when we are frequently immersed in the sounds of heaven, we are more likely to execute movements with greater accuracy and precision. At the end of the day, it is vitally important that we make consistent efforts to clearly hear the frequencies of heaven because these sounds provide us with revelation, knowledge, prophecy, and words of instruction, which can ultimately be embedded in our movement execution.

14 – Soundscapes of Worship: Spontaneous vs. Prophetic

As we explore the differences between spontaneous and prophetic sound, it is essential to remember that when we speak of sound, we are referring to song, music, mime, and any expression that influences atmospheres. Some of you encountering this for the first time might think that spontaneous and prophetic sounds are the same and perhaps use them interchangeably. However, they are distinct. Here, I define five principles that distinguish spontaneous sound from prophetic sound.

Principle 1: Spontaneous sound edifies self;
prophetic sound edifies the body of Christ.

If your worship leader, pastor, or preacher has ever directed a congregation to take a praise break, then that praise break is likely a response to some attribute of God or to the Word of God being preached. A praise break is classified as a spontaneous sound. It may even inspire others to join in, but the reasoning behind individual praise breaks is entirely independent because it is like speaking in tongues between you and God, not meant for others to understand. We will discuss more on prophetic sound and its ability to edify the body of Christ in the second principle.

Principle 2: Spontaneous sound is a movement inspired by a message but is not a manifestation of the message that inspired it; prophetic sound contains a message (revelation, knowledge, prophecy, or word of instruction) that manifests itself as a movement.

The message is the movement, and the movement is the message. As with the first principle, spontaneous sound is inspired by a message.

Principle 3: Spontaneous sound does not require interpretation or intelligibility; prophetic sound is eligible for interpretation or intelligibility.

Consider this: we do not need intellect to praise God. Even in Jesus's encounter with the woman at the well, He tells her that Samaritans worship what they do not know, while the Jews worship what they do know (John 4:22). There is a clear distinction that one can worship God without any intellectual basis. However, this is not an argument to prove that one sound is better than the other. I will address that issue separately.

Even though intellect is not a prerequisite for praising God, we are encouraged to pursue gifts, including the ability to prophesy or function prophetically. When you begin to prophesy or worship prophetically, your song, dance, motion, and artwork are all automatically subject to interpretation and intelligibility.

Principle 4: Spontaneous sound surpasses our understanding, while prophetic sound demands our understanding.

Just as with intellect, you do not need understanding to praise God, requiring minimal thought, discipline, and responsibility, thus making it spontaneous. The prophetic sound entails a higher degree of responsibility. If you are releasing a prophetic sound, you must understand how your gift operates. Even when one prophesies, the interpretation and understanding may not rest with the one who prophesies, but someone nearby may interpret the message embedded in an instrumental solo, a series of movements, or a piece of art. Understanding must be a requisite because a prophecy misunderstood might as well be dead. We know that God's Word does not fall to the ground as dead, but we also know that if a person does not seek to understand the promises presented to them through prophecy, the prophetic word or sound risks not manifesting or may exhibit a delayed manifestation in the life of the individual for whom the message was intended.

Principle 5: Spontaneous sound is already perfect; prophetic sound requires training and perfecting.

Scripture tells us that everything that has breath has the capacity to praise the Lord. We are instructed to make a joyful noise unto the Lord, implying that spontaneous sound is already perfect as creation participates in this praise. Spontaneous sound does not require the same level of discipline and training, as it is classified as a noise. One can discipline themselves to release a spontaneous sound unto the Lord, but the sound itself requires no additional training. For instance, I used to carry a worship timer that would buzz every seven minutes and twenty-seven seconds. Each time the buzzer went off, I would release a spontaneous praise to the Lord if it did not cause a distraction. (I would often wear this worship timer while at work). However, spontaneous sound does not carry the same responsibilities as prophetic sound. Releasing a prophetic sound requires training and perfecting. The gift to release a prophetic sound is perfect, but the skill, wisdom, and prudence required to release it are not perfect. It requires significant discipline to effectively use the gift of prophecy.

If you truly want to distinguish between the two types of sound, spontaneous sound does not require a direct translation of what you hear in the spirit. It is a personal response to what you sense spiritually, meant to create momentum for your personal breakthrough and no one else's. On the other hand, prophetic sound involves taking what you hear in the heavenly realms and finding the appropriate language and expression to release that word in this realm. Prophetic sound is a tool for edification and creates opportunities for breakthroughs for others, as it embodies the message from God meant to build up the body of Christ.

In summary, both spontaneous and prophetic sounds hold important places in worship. While spontaneous sound allows worship artists to express uninhibited praise, prophetic sound invites them to communicate God's messages for communal edification. Embracing the nuances of both can enhance the depth and impact of worship, offering enriched experiences for both the artist and the community.

15 – Sound Amplification

Amplification means "to expand on something, such as a statement, by the use of detail or illustration or by closer analysis" (Merriam-Webster Dictionary). Spontaneous sound can be beneficial, as it magnifies God because it is a response to His message. However, prophetic sound has the power to amplify and convey the message from the heart of God.

Music sounds more profound when melodies are in tune and in unison. Harmony enriches the melody, creating a fuller, richer sound. Yet, excessive complexity can transform a distinct sound into mere noise, failing to amplify the collective sound.

For worship artists, the essence of their art is more pronounced when there is unity, much like dancers following the same choreography or using the same instruments. This principle demonstrates why spontaneous sound or movement on its own may not always amplify a clear message. It highlights a unique communion with God within each artist. Diverse tongues bring diverse rhythms and movements, each with its language. Pure spontaneous worship to the Lord creates spontaneous noise, which is not inherently negative.

Which is Better? Spontaneous or Prophetic Sound

A common issue regarding prophetic and spontaneous worship is the misconception that one is superior. Some believe that music ministries focusing on one style are more effective than those that do not. However, Paul's warning to the Corinthians about being fascinated by gifts similarly applies to worship arts. One can engage in spontaneous worship without love, turning praise into mere entertainment or routine. Worship, whether spontaneous or prophetic, can fall into the trap of performance devoid of heartfelt love.

Both worship forms can devolve into noise lacking meaningful communication if elevated above other worship styles. Envying another artist's gifts, abilities, or expressions risks turning one's sound into a futile noise. Worship artists must remain enamored with God, rather than the gifts themselves.

Amplification by Fire

The reason why neither spontaneous nor prophetic worship is superior is that God amplifies sound and movement through His fire. When God desires a specific message to be heard, He baptizes it in fire, capturing attention regardless of its form. Consider Moses's encounter with the burning bush—its unconsumed state drew him in to receive God's message.

The day of Pentecost further illustrates this: with wind and tongues of fire, believers declared God's wonders in various languages. Though seemingly spontaneous, God amplified their words so those gathered from diverse nations could understand them.

Thus, whether worship is spontaneous or prophetic, if God anoints it with fire, the message within that worship will be supernaturally amplified. This divine fire speaks to the people suited to hear it, granting you a language and message that resonates with specific ethnicities, cultures, and life experiences. When someone identifies with your worship from a place of personal experience, God can set it aflame, igniting holy conversations and liberation through your worship.

16 – The Challenges of Navigating Spontaneous and Prophetic Sound

In the vibrant realm of worship arts, where singers, musicians, dancers, poets, and painters gather to amplify the divine message, understanding one's true identity and calling is paramount. This chapter delves into the nuanced distinction between spontaneous and prophetic worship. As worship artists, we are called not only to harness our creative gifts for God's glory but also to walk authentically and humbly within our artistic and spiritual communities. Through personal reflections and biblical insights, this chapter aims to illuminate the path of honoring God's voice in worship, emphasizing integrity, respect, and spiritual discernment. As we explore these themes, I invite you to reflect on your journey as a worship artist, allowing God to refine your purpose and elevate your gift in alignment with His perfect will.

Dealing with Imposters in Worship Arts

> *"Nevertheless, I have this against you: You tolerate that woman Jezebel, who calls herself a prophet. By her teaching, she misleads my servants into sexual immorality and the eating of food sacrificed to idols. I have given her time to repent of her immorality, but she is unwilling." (Revelation 2:20-21, NIV)*

In the world of worship arts, too many claim identities that don't align with their true gifts, revealing a spirit akin to Jezebel. When individuals exalt themselves to titles or positions without genuine authority, they risk misleading others. It's crucial to recognize that using certain gifts does not automatically grant one the authority to hold a specific position or title. Sadly, this misunderstanding often leads to a lack of respect for worship artists within the church, where many are mislabeled as prophetic when they are simply engaging in spontaneous worship.

As a spontaneous musician, I understand that improvisation can be taught and is relatively easy for those with musical training. I studied jazz in school, where improvisation was a fundamental skill. However, prophetic playing is different. Before stepping into the musician's pit or during worship, I ask God, "What would you like for me to play?" Even if I've rehearsed a piece countless times, I remain open to God's direction, asking, "Is there anything you want me to play differently today?" This openness to divine inspiration transforms my music into a prophetic expression, releasing God's messages from His eternal repertoire.

In worship, spontaneous praise is valuable, but not all spontaneous acts are prophetic. Once, I engaged in a series of Facebook livestreams, closing each session by waving swing flags. Many labeled me as a flagger, but I clarified that I'm simply a worshipper using flags as instruments of expression, not prophecy. My role isn't prophetic flagging, as I lack the skill for such a designation. Despite this, I know I'm anointed to release prophetic sounds—a gift activated in me by a prophetic mentor.

Meanwhile, some individuals boastfully identify as the "spontaneous sect," without recognizing the difference between spontaneous and prophetic worship. This confusion requires education rather than condemnation. Worship artists—be they musicians, singers, dancers, or others—must understand the distinction between spontaneous and prophetic worship and be prepared to seek forgiveness from church leaders and fellow ministers if they've misrepresented themselves.

Respect within ministry is paramount. We must remain honest about our identities and avoid behaviors that might brand us as hypocrites. Pride and arrogance have no place in worship, so it's essential to let God address these issues within us.

The Sound of Worship Being Silenced

When worship team members seem to stifle your prophetic expressions, entrust the matter to God. Seek His guidance on how your prophetic gift fits within the body of Christ, always adhering to church order.

During one service, a fellow musician told me to stop playing, despite having no authority to do so. Although tempted to respond harshly, I chose to avoid confrontation by leaving the musician's pit. Later, the musician reached out to discuss the incident. To prevent potential conflict, I suggested a three-way conversation with a higher authority. Ultimately, the musician approached the pastor independently, realized his mistake, and apologized, preserving our relationship and reinforcing trust.

This experience underscores the importance of surrendering conflict to God. Allow Him to handle situations respectfully and righteously. Whether labeled as spontaneous or prophetic, always remain humble and aligned with church structure, avoiding the temptation to assert authority unjustly. Through humility and deference to God's will, room will be made for your gifts as He sees fit.

At the end of the day, it's not about the title or position you hold but about being a true vessel for God's message. Whether you consider yourself a spontaneous or prophetic worship artist, it's important to operate within the boundaries and authority established by your community and church leaders. This ensures that your contributions to worship are both edifying and respectful, allowing the spiritual gifts given to you to shine through in a way that honors God and strengthens the body of Christ.

By maintaining humility and openness to God's guidance, you allow Him to create opportunities for your artistic expressions to impact others meaningfully. Trust that He will make room for your gifts as He deems necessary, leading not only to personal growth but also fostering unity and respect among fellow worship artists and the congregation. Thus, navigate your role in worship arts with integrity and a sincere heart, always seeking to glorify God above all else.

17 – The Truth Concerning Holy Spirit and Tongues

"And these signs will follow those who believe: In My name they will cast out demons; they will speak with new tongues" (Mark 16:17, NKJV).

Warning: This teaching might offend you, especially if you love your spiritual gifts more than Christ's teachings. It's time to settle the debate once and for all concerning the argument about the Holy Spirit and tongues. The reason I must bring up this topic is that tongues are unmistakably one of the ways we release heaven's frequencies into the earth. There is a sect of Christianity that believes speaking in tongues is one of the primary pieces of evidence that a person is filled with the Holy Spirit. The first problem with this argument is that there are too many offended and illiterate people giving incomplete interpretations of this scripture. The second problem is that we've given more honor to later New Testament concepts that are contrary to Christ's nature. We tend to give greater honor to things that Jesus did not explicitly teach than to what he actually taught.

In Mark's Gospel, Jesus reveals that people will speak in tongues, but he never explicitly links this with the Holy Spirit. It's implied, yet as a teacher, I ask: Why did Jesus leave out the Holy Spirit in that statement? It's simple – this isn't a teaching but a promise of what's to come. Jesus likely didn't mention the Holy Spirit to avoid tongues being misused as the sole evidence of His presence, which might lead to excluding members of the body of Christ. In fact, Jesus rarely discusses the Holy Spirit in the Gospels. His main teaching on the topic is in John 16, occurring before Mark 16:17.

> "But now I go away to Him who sent Me, and none of you asks Me, 'Where are You going?' But because I have said these things to you, sorrow has filled your heart. Nevertheless, I tell you the truth. It is to your advantage that I go away: for if I do not go away, the Helper will not come to you; but if I depart, I will send Him to you. And when He has come, He will convict the world of sin, and of righteousness, and of judgment: of sin, because they do not believe in Me; of righteousness, because I go to My Father and you see Me no more; of judgment, because the ruler of this world is judged.
>
> "I still have many things to say to you, but you cannot bear them now. However, when He, the Spirit of truth, has come, He will guide you into all truth; for He will not speak on His own authority, but whatever He hears He will speak; and He will tell you things to come. He will glorify Me, for He will take of what is Mine and declare it to you. All things that the Father has are Mine. Therefore, I said that He will take of Mine and declare it to you" (John 16:5-15, NKJV).

In John 16, Jesus teaches that the Holy Spirit's main role is to challenge and correct our beliefs, replacing errors with the truth about the Father and Jesus. This introduction to the Holy Spirit sets the foundation. Other teachings are secondary revelations about the Spirit's attributes and roles. Notice how today, worship often calls on the Holy Spirit for miracles rather than guidance in truth.

We, as the church, for some reason honor Paul's teachings over Jesus's teachings. We must understand that Paul's teachings about the Holy Spirit are a later fulfillment of what Jesus originally taught about the Holy Spirit. Jesus never specifically talked about the Holy Spirit and speaking in tongues in the same breath. Paul's teachings on spiritual gifts will never receive greater honor than Jesus's teachings on the Holy Spirit. Paul's teachings on the Holy Spirit are a greater work that Jesus could not speak of at the time. Also, because we tend to make erroneous associations, we must understand that just because you do greater work doesn't mean you get greater honor. Those two things are independent of one another.

Jesus wanted us to focus on righteousness, not the gifts. Righteousness isn't fulfilled through tongues or spiritual gifts but through the Spirit's conviction. Immature believers might try convincing you otherwise, but these teachings point you back to Christ, away from merely fleshly worship. What I'm really trying to get is that if speaking in tongues is so important to Jesus, he would have taught about it while he was in the earth, and the Holy Spirit would have inspired one of the four writers of the gospels to include speaking in tongues as one of Jesus's teachings. Jesus commissioned his apostles to make disciples and teach them to obey everything that he has commanded. Jesus never commanded us to speak in tongues; tongues is a gift, not a commandment. Jesus also said that whoever teaches others to obey the commands in the sermon on the mount will be called great in the kingdom of heaven. There is absolutely no other teaching or commandment that any man can teach that has the power to make a person great in the kingdom. So why do we keep arguing about teachings on speaking in tongues? It's because speaking in tongues edifies us and makes us feel great, and it is in our nature to want to feel great! The reason why our the efficacy of our worship arts has not reached maximum throttle is because we spend too much time arguing about not just tongues, but everything in the bible that does not make us great in God's kingdom.

I don't intend to discredit speaking in tongues. It's important to recognize its role in accessing heaven's frequencies, especially when you consider these scriptures:

> *However, we speak wisdom among those who are mature, yet not the wisdom of this age, nor of the rulers of this age, who are coming to nothing. But we speak the wisdom of God in a mystery, the hidden wisdom which God ordained before the ages for our glory, which none of the rulers of this age knew; for had they known, they would not have crucified the Lord of glory.*
>
> *But as it is written: "Eye has not seen, nor ear heard, Nor have entered into the heart of man The things which God has prepared for those who love Him."*
>
> *But God has revealed them to us through His Spirit. For the Spirit searches all things, yes, the deep things of God. For what man knows the things of a man except the spirit of the man which is in him? Even so no one knows the things of God except the Spirit of God. Now we have received, not the spirit of the world, but the Spirit who is from God, that we might know the things that have been freely given to us by God.*

Continue speaking in tongues, as it refreshes and activates other spiritual gifts. Speaking in tongues is what enables us to search the heart and mind of God that other methods cannot. Many believers have powerful testimonies about tongues' impact on their lives and ministries. Yet, tongues should not become an idol. I must say this because some of us have been deeply wounded because you might fellowship in a church that does not share an accurate interpretation of Paul's instruction about tongues, prophecy, and other spiritual gifts. For you to have easier access to heaven's hidden frequencies, those wounds that you have about tongues and spiritual gifts need to be healed with the truth. Worship should be in Spirit and truth, not just spirit and tongues. We can worship in tongues or our language and still be distant from God's truth, which is in Jesus. If the Corinthian church did not struggle with this, Paul would never have addressed it, and we would not have any written insight into the spiritual gifts from an apostle. So, his instruction on spiritual gifts is extremely important, just not the center of our Christian faith.

As a church, we've mistakenly used tongues to measure spirituality when they are simply a manifestation. Jesus said tongues would follow believers, not just disciples. Being a believer and being a disciple are distinct; Jesus defined disciples as those who abide in His word. A disciple's quality is measured by their adherence to the word, not by their gift of tongues. God judges the conversation and the insights from tongues, now available through the Holy Spirit. Without interpretation, we cannot gauge tongues' power. Worship leaders may navigate earthly frequencies but miss spiritual alignment with God and his word. Don't let natural sounds deceive you about God or others. God made tongues complex to keep us reliant on His understanding.

Paul teaches that spiritual gifts, including tongues, should ultimately serve to edify the body of Christ. The greater spiritual virtues beyond tongues and prophecy are faith, hope, and love. Faith involves believing the true testimony of God; hope is confidently expecting God's promises; love is valuing others as God does. Without these, there's a risk of misaligning with heaven's frequencies. Worship should focus on faith, hope, and love to remain pleasing to God. Though the church excels in believing God's promises and loving as He does, we must allow the Holy Spirit to strengthen our faith to access heaven's frequencies through worship.

In summary, while speaking in tongues is vital, it should not overshadow the core of our faith—living in the Spirit and truth. Tongues is a gift meant for edification, but our journey of faith is ultimately measured by how we embody Christ's teachings in love and truth.

18 – The Sound of Motion

In a world resonating with visible and invisible frequencies, worship artists—singers, dancers, musicians, poets, and painters—are uniquely positioned to tap into the intricate tapestry of sound and movement. This chapter delves into the profound impact of both audible and inaudible sounds, illustrating how they transcend human perception to influence spiritual realms. By exploring the science behind sound frequencies and their interaction with movement, we uncover new dimensions of prophetic expression and authority in worship. As you journey through these concepts, consider how your artistic expressions serve as conduits for divine interaction, harnessing the power to shape atmospheres and connect with the eternal.

Inaudible Sound

Sound does not have to be heard by your ear to have an impact. Every creature is designed to hear certain frequencies of sound, but human hearing is limited to certain frequencies. Thus, there are two types of frequencies that are outside our hearing range: infrasound and ultrasound.

Let's define these inaudible sounds to humans. Keep in mind that our perception of sound is relative to human hearing. Infrasound has a low frequency and a long wavelength, allowing these sounds to travel longer distances. Elephants, for instance, have more than one type of communication. We often think of their high-pitched roars, but they can also communicate through vibrations in the earth, which travel over miles.

Ultrasound, however, has a high frequency but a short wavelength, traveling shorter distances and being more easily disrupted. Consider a pregnant woman receiving an ultrasound. Why is gel applied to the body before using ultrasound? Each medium can carry sound differently. Ultrasound does not travel well through air but does so excellently in liquids. Because air can disrupt its travel, gel is used to ensure the signal reaches the body effectively, producing a clear image. Even if the human ear cannot hear these sounds, science confirms their existence.

One practical example of movement impacting sound is the cricket. I once lived in an apartment frequently visited by crickets during the transition from summer to fall in the United States. Approaching a cricket casually would likely scare it away, but moving slowly helped in getting closer. Crickets detect air movement with hairs that sense vibrations, allowing them to respond to our presence.

Knowing crickets react to the sound of my movements, I devised my own method to catch them using a vacuum cleaner. Its loud noise can mask movement sounds, increasing the chance of capturing them. Hand-eye coordination is still key, as crickets can eventually sense the vacuum hose's movement.

If crickets can hear and respond to our movements, how much more is possible with heavenly hosts and demons when we operate in our authority in Christ! Our movements have influence. When an officer raises a badge, it signals authority and calls for submission. In spiritual matters, our expressions in worship, whether through song or dance, can shape the atmosphere. If our spiritual movements don't elicit a response, it may indicate a lack of authority or other factors impacting the atmosphere. A difference exists between having faith to shift atmospheres and possessing the authority to do so.

Audible Sound

Now that we've explored inaudible sounds, let's return to those within the human hearing range. Movement can create audible sounds as well. For example, a lion tamer's whip commands authority and can intimidate. For many, the sound of a parent's disciplinary tool prepares us for receiving instruction.

The buzzing of insects stems from the rapid movement of their wings. Their wings move at such a high frequency that we can't hear them from afar, but they become audible when closer.

When playing instruments like the recorder, the movement and placement of fingers alter the air passage, thereby influencing the note frequency. Even on a windy day, as air moves through branches, the rustling leaves can be heard, akin to the praises of creation.

At the end of the day, all movement creates sound, regardless of its scale. So, worship artists who aspire to master their movements: you have the influence over creation and beyond, extending even into the heavenly realms.

19 - The Search for Hidden Frequencies

This chapter delves into the profound concept of worship as both a spiritual weapon and a pathway to unlocking heaven's hidden frequencies. Grounded in biblical insights from Matthew 11 and the story of Jericho, it challenges us to reconsider how we approach worship and revelation. By exploring the intersection of silence, consecration, and artistic expression, we uncover the transformative power of truly seeking rest in Christ. Through personal experiences and scientific research, the chapter invites readers on a journey to deepen their spiritual practice, discovering the divine sounds and revelations accessible in moments of diligent pursuit and quiet contemplation.

In the beginning of Matthew 11, John's messengers question whether Jesus is truly the Messiah. Jesus responds by detailing the miracles that have occurred since he began his public ministry. He then compares this generation to a crowd too distracted to notice children performing music meant to inspire rejoicing and lament. Essentially, Jesus illustrates that this generation, despite witnessing miracles, remains unrepentant. He praises the Father for concealing the kingdom of heaven from those who see themselves as wise and revealing it to those with childlike hearts. Jesus concludes by stating that he is the gateway to revelation, encouraging people to seek rest from their weary labors.

While God may still perform miracles, He conceals the kingdom from those who remain unrepentant. Similarly, heaven's hidden frequencies are withheld from those unwilling to earnestly pursue rest from their unfruitful works. Our worship should originate from a place of rest, where God chooses to reveal hidden truths through Christ Jesus. I propose that many worship arts ministries strive for heavenly music, choreography, and other forms of prophetic artistry. Yet, I offer biblical, scientific, and anecdotal evidence that these heavenly frequencies must be diligently sought.

The Jericho Jigsaw Puzzle

Are you familiar with the story of the walls of Jericho falling as Israel releases a shout? Perhaps you've heard teachings suggesting our worship can similarly break down walls. While this may hold some truth, this revelation is often passed down without thorough understanding. It is fragmented and incomplete. Will you allow me to bring clarity?

The issue with this particular revelation about worship is the assumption that we inherently possess the authority to release a sound that will automatically defeat strongholds. But have you ever been asked when you last consecrated yourself for six or more days before a worship set? If we surveyed worship teams, we'd find that most do not regularly engage in such deliberate consecration. Yes, the walls of Jericho fell on the seventh day as they shouted, but Israel had spent six days in silence, searching for the sound to destroy the wall. While they may not have known it, as they circled Jericho quietly, they were seeking a hidden frequency in the silence.

Let's discuss the Hebrew word for silence, "d'mamah." The first letter, daleth, signifies a door or pathway. The next two letters, mem, mean waters or chaos, and the final letter, hey, implies revelation. Thus, "d'mamah" can be seen as a picture of God parting the Red Sea for Israel, revealing a path through chaos. Similarly, to find revelation and heaven's hidden frequencies, we must seek the path amid chaos.

Dancing in the Dark

In my research, I found an article on the effects of dance on dancers' brains as they acquire skills and techniques (Sevdalis, V., & Keller, P. E., "Captured by motion: Dance, action understanding, and social cognition," Brain and cognition, 2011). An intriguing observation was the advantage of dancing in silence or out of synchrony with music. The research indicated that dancers become less reliant on predictable patterns, discovering movements in silence and forming new anticipatory cues normally unattainable when synchronized with music. This search for choreography allows dancers to convey unique visual messages. If the secular dance world can apply these principles, how much more should the body of Christ?

Worship teams frequently imitate musical and physical expressions without innovation. It's frustrating when performers mimic original songs too closely, down to specific ad-libs. Spontaneous or prophetic phrases are often discovered or stumbled upon, not merely copied. I find it disrespectful for artists to imitate and expect the same anointing as the original.

Worship teams should occasionally imitate, but should ultimately seek the frequencies God created. While some claim to destroy strongholds through worship, often they attempt to create a sound without investing time in seeking heaven's hidden frequencies.

Pursuing Heavenly Frequencies

> *Father, I ask for the release of worship songs that come from the throne room in heaven, for these songs have been birth straight from your glory, a place where time does not exist. I desire to be in sync with the sounds and vibrations that holds me together.*
>
> *Allow this worship to remove me from the confines of time and into my birthplace where your glorious works are seen. Through this amazing worship, allow me to engage in the works that yield food that endures to eternal life.*
>
> *You have prepared songs so that I might enter into the beauty of your holiness. Therefore, establish your eternal dwelling place not built by human hands inside of me by giving me the songs of eternity! Because the songs are birth from eternity, let me participate in the eternity of the worship at your throne!*

Drawing from personal testimony, I have found that God reveals heaven's frequencies when you search between chaos. In years 2013 and 2014, I spent a year and a half rising at 3:00 am to sit in silence, read, and pray as inspired by scriptures. At

5:00 am, I'd return to bed and rise again for work at 7:00 am. During this, I prayed to hear melodies played in heaven, using those exact words that opened this chapter. As you can see, that prayer simple and drastically different from the prayer from the chapter entitled, "Approaching Worship in Anticipation". Anyway, about eight months in, I had a dream featuring music, which I recorded and practiced on my electric saxophone. God named the melody "the light of the knowledge of the glory displayed in the face of Christ" (2 Corinthians 4:6).

On Friday night, during a Good Friday worship service, the worship leader adjusted the mood of the chord progressions for prophetic playing. I realized the music from my dream fit perfectly. Despite my nerves, I started with some spontaneous notes and transitioned into the melody from the dream. It was an extraordinary experience in prophetic worship, and I recorded it on my phone. Afterwards, several people remarked that they sensed the lightning and thunder of the throne room as I played. That night, God confirmed to me that my prayer for prophetic sounds had been answered.

This experience taught me that prophetic melodies can be revealed through the practice of silence. It took ten years to recognize the process and articulate how the hidden frequencies of heaven are discovered: through vigorously seeking rest in Christ. This pursuit allows us to hear these divine frequencies, demonstrating that commitment to spiritual discipline and seeking God's presence can reveal profound insights and artistic expressions.

Whenever I get a chance to play my electric saxophone with worship teams, there are two consistent practices that I carry with me. If there is a specific set list, I mentally rehearse melodies and countermelodies in silence when I'm not listening to the songs. Even if I have physically and mentally rehearsed a song, I recognize that I must still ask God how he wants me to proceed to play in worship. Therefore, my second practice occurs during live worship sets; I have learned to sit and search for the empty spaces or silent spaces in the song. Sometimes, God gives me nothing new to play and allows me to continue and flow as I see fit or as rehearsed, but I've learned to never deny God the courtesy of how he wants to reveal himself through the playing of my instrument.

Finally, when you become more familiar with the frequencies that God allows you hear, eventually you will begin to identify pieces of music and song selections that you know were inspired by heaven without a shadow of a doubt. I do not want to give a list of songs as an example to avoid showing bias. Heaven's hidden frequencies are best discovered than explicitly given away as a commodity. But if you value this testimony, I can say that I've been able to identify specific arrangements and intervals of notes in other pieces of music that God had given to me in my prior time. When you discover that God has shared these same frequencies with other worship artists, you will recognize that them not only by their musical arrangement, but also by the context of the song and the underlying message that is conveyed or assigned by God to such frequencies. These confirmations are not for us to monopolize or make a commodity out of those frequencies, but rather to humble us knowing that we are not the origin of those frequencies; God is.

20 – Worship Authority and Responsibility

The concept of authority is prominently featured in the book of Ephesians, where God establishes Jesus as an authority over all powers and dominions. This divine framework extends to the Church, the body of Christ, which is called to exercise this authority. Through the five-fold ministry, Jesus empowers the Church to grow and mature in its authoritative role. This authority within the Christian community is evident in various relationships: wives and husbands, parents and children, and slaves and masters, each displaying an authoritative balance of respect and love to maintain dominion over forces that seek to divide.

For worship artists, this theme of authority carries a significant responsibility. Worship, especially through music with psalms, hymns, and spiritual songs, is not merely an art form—it's a powerful expression of dominion over darkness and sin. This art form holds the responsibility of nurturing gratitude and obedience among believers. It serves as a means to expose darkness, enlighten others with God's wisdom, and dominate over sinful behaviors such as sexual immorality and greed.

The often overlooked aspect of worship is its role in exposing darkness and teaching believers to exercise dominion over it. As worship artists, you are tasked with illuminating these truths through your music. In a contemporary context where musical expressions often circle around darkness, there's a need to creatively confront and lead congregations towards repentance—a potent form of power that precedes all others.

Repentance should precede the pursuit of signs, wonders, and spiritual gifts. Jesus promised that signs would follow those who believe; yet, the pursuit of signs often overshadows the pursuit of His teachings and righteousness. Therefore, as worship artists, it's crucial to emphasize making disciples through your music, rather than merely amassing followers. This discipleship requires a sound of repentance that resonates across the earth, realigning the focus from surface-level expressions of power to the humble strength found in genuine repentance and discipleship.

In summary, your role as worship artists is to harness the authority granted by God, using your creative gifts to expose darkness, inspire repentance, and cultivate a deeper understanding of spiritual dominion among believers. Through this, you fulfill your responsibility of making true disciples who are rooted in the teachings of Jesus and His kingdom.

21 – The Resonant Frequency

As we come to the end of our journey, let's take a moment to recap. We've delved into the origins of worship and explored the struggles we've faced as God's children in maintaining authenticity, especially within the realm of prophetic worship. Through our exploration, we've examined how God created sound and challenged some of the sacred traditions we've established in our worship experiences. This includes evaluating worship as a weapon and considering how the presentation of lyrics and themes in our expressions of worship impacts the maturity of the body of Christ.

Throughout this journey, I've shared personal experiences to inspire you to search for heaven's hidden frequencies. In doing so, we've also addressed the hurt and pain experienced by prophetic worship artists in their quest to discover these frequencies.

As we conclude this exploration, I want to present the argument for what I believe to be the dominant or resonant frequency hidden in heaven that we must anchor ourselves to: the frequency of repentance. Consider this as we turn our attention to the future events outlined in the book of Revelation. Allow me to reframe our understanding of Revelation. I previously mentioned that creation is designed to respond to the sons of God. When contemplating Jesus's birth, the earthly realm responded to Jesus by clothing Him in flesh. Similarly, as we study Revelation, particularly chapters 1-4, we see heaven responding to a fully revealed Jesus as a spirit-being with human-like features. Heaven adorns Jesus with white hair like wool, eyes like fire, feet like brass, among other attributes. In Revelation 5, heaven presents Jesus as a lamb worthy to break the seals on the scroll, illustrating how both heaven and earth react to Him. Thus, if we genuinely seek the hidden frequencies of heaven, they are likely found within Revelation 1-5.

Repentance remains crucial to Jesus in the book of Revelation and will continue to be so until His return. Despite the passage of 2000 years, Jesus's message is unchanged. This prompts reflection: why do we, as believers, act as though regular encounters with repentance are unnecessary? Let us remind ourselves of Jesus's appeals to five of the seven churches:

- Ephesus needs to repent for their spiritual apathy.
- Pergamum needs to repent for their faith in compromised teachings and idols.
- Thyatira needs to repent for their immorality and compromised faith in false teachings.
- Sardis needs to repent for losing confidence in who God is, His power, and what He has promised to do with His power on their behalf.
- Laodicea needs to repent for their pride and spiritual blindness.

Amid our efforts to discern which church we belong to in Revelation, we often overlook the enduring call for repentance within His church until the end of the age. The church's origins are rooted in repentance, a foundational truth we must never forget. Moreover, heaven's resonance with Jesus's teachings aligns beautifully with His desire for heaven and earth to become one. It is logical that He would release messages that converge upon one another.

To substantiate the idea that heaven resonates with Jesus and His teachings, we can look to both the admonishments to the churches in Revelation and the principles outlined in the Sermon on the Mount, demonstrating that the nature of heaven closely aligns with Jesus' voice and message. Here's how this argument can be developed:

1. Heaven Reflects Jesus' Call to Righteousness

In the Sermon on the Mount, Jesus outlines a blueprint for heavenly living, centered on righteousness, humility, and love. Heaven is a place of perfect righteousness, devoid of sin, corruption, and hypocrisy. The teachings in Matthew 5-7 exemplify a life that mirrors the purity and holiness of heaven, aligning with Jesus' warnings in Revelation for the churches to repent and live righteously. Heaven echoes Jesus' call for repentance and restoration, urging the churches to return to their first love and cautioning them against spiritual complacency.

2. Heaven Speaks of Endurance and Faithfulness

In both Revelation and the Sermon on the Mount, Jesus emphasizes endurance and faithfulness. Revelation 2:10 and Matthew 5:10-12 reveal a heaven that values steadfastness amidst persecution. There is no room for fear or compromise in heaven. The promise of crowns, rewards, and eternal life for those who overcome and remain faithful underscores Jesus' call for perseverance. His teachings to love enemies and pray for persecutors highlight the kind of heart that will be fully realized in heaven, where suffering for righteousness' sake is honored.

3. Heaven is Free from Hypocrisy and Lukewarm Faith

Jesus' rebuke of hypocrisy, both in Revelation and the Sermon on the Mount, emphasizes a heaven marked by purity and authenticity. The rebuke of the Laodiceans for being lukewarm (Revelation 3:15-16) and Sardis for appearing alive yet being dead inside (Revelation 3:1) parallels His criticism of outward displays of righteousness without true inward transformation (Matthew 6:1-18). Heaven is therefore a place of genuine faith, where hypocrisy and superficiality cannot exist. The atmosphere of heaven consistently reflects Jesus' call for truth and sincerity, perfectly aligning with His desire for integrity in faith.

4. Heaven Offers the Reward for Overcoming Temptation and Sin

Both Revelation and the Sermon on the Mount address overcoming temptations and challenges. Jesus promises rewards to the overcomers in Revelation, such as eating from the tree of life and ruling with Christ (Revelation 2:7, 3:21), reflecting the ultimate rewards of heaven. Similarly, the Sermon on the Mount challenges believers to take radical actions against sin (Matthew 5:29-30), highlighting the eternal rewards for those who do so. Heaven thus embodies Jesus' encouragement to overcome sin and temptation, offering eternal rewards to those who have triumphed in life through righteousness.

5. Heaven is a Place of Promised Blessings

The Beatitudes (Matthew 5:3-12) highlight blessings promised to those who embody the characteristics of the Kingdom of Heaven, such as being poor in spirit, merciful, and pure in heart. These blessings align with the promises Jesus makes to the faithful churches in Revelation (Revelation 2-3), where overcoming leads to eternal life, hidden manna, and reigning with Christ. The sound of heaven is abundant with these fulfilled promises—blessings for those who have lived according to Jesus' teachings.

Conclusion: Heaven Echoes Jesus' Teachings

In both the Sermon on the Mount and the letters to the churches in Revelation, Jesus lays out values, behaviors, and attitudes that align with heaven. Heaven is where these teachings come to full fruition—where righteousness is rewarded, where faithfulness through trials is celebrated, and where hypocrisy is absent. The admonishments to the churches and the moral imperatives of the Sermon on the Mount reveal that **Heaven sounds like Jesus** because His teachings form the very heart of what heaven upholds: righteousness, faithfulness, purity, and the ultimate reward for overcoming sin.

The Final Plea for Heaven's Hidden Frequencies

In the end, we are called to worship in Spirit and in truth. The longer we deny that Jesus is still seeking a church that lives a lifestyle of repentance for not fully adhering to His commands, the more I fear for church members who may lose their way. This may happen because of their passionate pursuit of the sounds and frequencies of heaven, rather than the frequencies of Jesus's heart. I hope the messages in this work have brought you to a greater level of spiritual sobriety in your Christian walk, ensuring your pursuit of deeper and more intimate expressions of worship is continually purified from this moment forward.

Based on the information presented, since heaven's hidden frequencies are tied to repentance and Jesus's teachings, can we encourage modern-day worship leaders and true psalmists to write songs about forgiveness and repentance? Can worship leaders and psalmists create songs that encapsulate the teachings of the Sermon on the Mount, rather than focusing solely on miracles, signs, and wonders? The church has become proficient in the latter, yet we remain mediocre in the one thing that Jesus said would make us the greatest in the kingdom! We have excelled in singing about signs and wonders but have neglected songs that root us in faith, like hymns that remind us of our need for repentance, which is essentially what the Sermon on the Mount emphasizes. Our worship has been filled with lyrics that teach about God's promises, but we have few songs that disciple us in all that Jesus commanded.

Do we need further proof that we are no longer captivated by the sound of repentance? Many newer worship songs focus on signs, wonders, fire, and wind. While these themes are important, have we forgotten the process Jesus led His disciples through before they witnessed fire and wind? They underwent years of repentance, and perhaps anything set on fire without repentance is strange fire to God. Jesus wanted His people to be captivated by the sound of repentance before He sent them the sound of a rushing wind.

Romans 11:29 warns us that gifts and callings are without repentance. God, as a good Father, will not revoke His gifts, but according to the Son, we are expected to leave our gifts at the altar. If we love our gifts to the point of ignoring our need for repentance and are irresponsible in our relationships, it is only a matter of time before our Father disciplines us. Thus, I propose to worship artists and leaders that an unrepentant heart set on fire is a strange fire. An unrepentant heart tested by fire cannot have the same lasting effect as a repentant one. I pray we do not allow our gifts to deceive us into thinking that repentance is no longer necessary. Instead, may we embrace repentance as a pathway to authentic worship that resonates with the true heart of Jesus and the harmonious frequencies of heaven.

Concluding Prayer

Father, I praise and thank You for being the One who created all things. I thank You for creating worship before the foundations of the earth and creating a plan for us to be divine participants in worshipping You with all our heart, mind, soul, and strength through the sacrifice of Your Son, Jesus. I thank You for giving us Your Spirit so that we can understand what it means to worship You in Spirit and in truth to enable us to partner with You in subduing the earth.

Father, I pray that You would continue to give revelatory knowledge of Jesus Christ to myself and all those who will follow these teachings in dance musicality. I pray that everyone who follows these teachings will humbly embrace these truths so that they may experience greater measures of the power associated with developing a worshipful lifestyle, whether it is in music, dance, mime, ministry, business, or career work. May we all be captivated by Christ so that our sound may be clear and uncontaminated, and all creation can rejoice with us as we worship. May we cast down any thought and imagination that exalts itself against the knowledge of You so that we can become properly constructed temples for your Holy Spirit. May we develop a cloud consciousness that will help us turn from the temptations of sin and embrace the weight of Your glory, that we can endure in our faith toward You.

We thank and praise You for allowing us to carry and emit the heaven's hidden frequencies so that we might go forth and liberate all creation through the power of the gospel of Jesus Christ! It is in the name of Jesus that we pray; amen!

Bibliography

Dolmetsch Online Music Dictionary. 2015a. Articulation. http://www. dolmetsch.com/defst1.htm (accessed January 9, 2021).

———. 2015b. Canon. http://www.dolmetsch.com/defst1.htm (accessed January 9, 2021).

———. 2015c. Rhythmic variation. http://www.dolmetsch.com/ defst1.htm (accessed January 9, 2021).

Grant, L., 2017. Enhancing Musicality in Ballet Technique Classes. *Dance Education in Practice*, *3*(3), pp.20-26.

Kuhn, L. 1999. Beat. In *Baker's student encyclopedia of music.* Vol. 1, A-G, ed. L. Kuhn, 99. New York: Schirmer Reference.

Latham, A. 2002. Tempo. In *The Oxford companion to music,* ed. A. Latham. New York: Oxford University Press.

Randel, D. 1986. Meter. In *The new Harvard dictionary of music,* ed. D. Randel, 489. Cambridge, MA: Belknap.

Sevdalis, V., & Keller, P. E. (2011). Captured by motion: Dance, action understanding, and social cognition. Brain and cognition, 77(2), 231-236.

About the Author

EUAL PHILLIPS is a Renaissance Systems Thinker and Teacher with a unique blend of expertise and passion. With a background in biomedical engineering and a career as a secondary math and science teacher, he skillfully merges biblical, spiritual, and scientific principles to forge groundbreaking philosophies, teachings, and prayers that address intricate challenges at their core. Eual's dedication extends to the world of worship arts, where he excels as an electronic wind controller specialist and recording artist. His critical thinking skills are also used as a curriculum specialist and instructor at the Christ Center for Dance and the Arts.

In his role as an educator, Eual creatively applies his biomedical science background by adapting laboratory experiments for high school students. He skillfully demonstrates how science is intricately intertwined with every facet of their present and future lives, influencing the evolution of their identities, beliefs, and values. His ultimate aspiration is to nurture a generation of student scientists who recognize the profound societal impact their innovative research ideas can bring about. Eual Phillips is a true visionary, seamlessly bridging the worlds of education, science, faith, and art to inspire transformative change.

Follow Eual on Social Media!

YouTube:
Academic Intercession
www.youtube.com/@prayerforschools

Facebook:
www.facebook.com/eualphillips.min/

Instagram: www.instagram.com/eual_phillips_edu/

TikTok:
www.tiktok.com/@eualaphillips

Additional Books by the Author

- The Scribal Responsibility: Salt, Light, and the Pursuit of Social Justice (2023)
- Shifting Atmospheres in Worship: Advanced Theory and Application (2021)

To see the entire collection, visit:
amazon.com/author/eaphillips.